Central Asian Republics

MICHAEL KORT

Facts On File, Inc.

For Alex and Roni, the newest arrivals

Facts On File, Inc.
132 West 31st Street
New York NY 10001

Library of Congress Cataloging-in-Publication Data

Kort, Michael.
   Central Asian Republics / Michael Kort.
      p. cm. — (Nations in transition)
   Includes bibliographical references and index.
   ISBN 0-8160-5074-0
   1. Asia, Central—History. I. Title. II. Series.
   DK856.K67 2003   *04/04*
   958—dc21   2003049031

Facts On File books are available at special discounts when purchased in bulk quantities for businesses, associations, institutions, or sales promotions. Please call our Special Sales Department in New York at (212) 967-8800 or (800) 322-8755.

You can find Facts On File on the World Wide Web at
http://www.factsonfile.com

Text design by Erika K. Arroyo
Cover design by Nora Wertz
Maps by Pat Meschino © Facts On File

Printed in the United States of America

MP FOF 10 9 8 7 6 5 4 3 2 1

This book is printed on acid-free paper.

CONTENTS

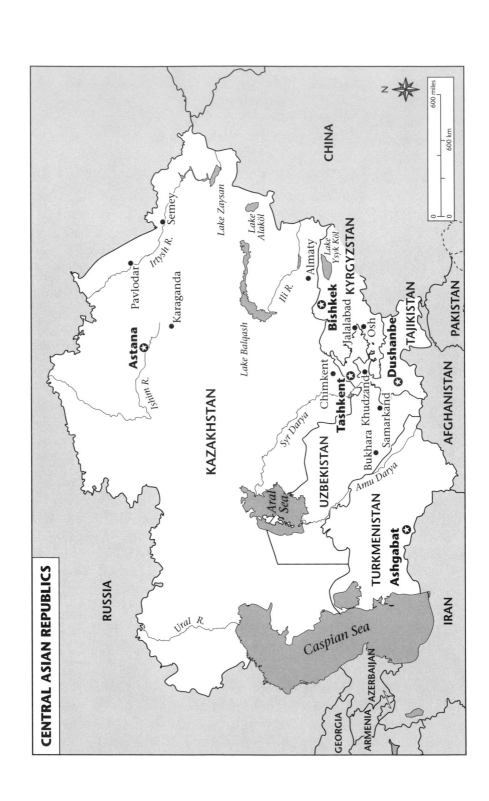

CENTRAL ASIAN REPUBLICS

INTRODUCTION

When the Soviet Union collapsed in 1991, the largest country on earth crumbled into 15 independent states. Each new country corresponded to one of the previous republics of the Soviet Union. Because the Soviet Union spanned northern Eurasia from the Baltic Sea to the Pacific Ocean, some of those new countries were situated in Europe, while others were in Asia. By far the best known and most important of the successor states was Russia, the core of the former Soviet empire. A sprawling, autocratic empire for more than two centuries before the Bolshevik Revolution of 1917, Russia's roots reached back more than 1,000 years. After the 1991 collapse, it retained about three-quarters of the Soviet Union's territory and, therefore, kept its status as the world's largest country. While historically and culturally European, Russia, like the former Soviet Union, spanned the breadth of Eurasia.

Other, less familiar European parts of the former Soviet Union were Ukraine, Belarus, Lithuania, Latvia, and Moldova. Most important in geopolitical terms was Ukraine, located to Russia's southwest and close to the geographic center of Europe. Ukraine was Europe's second-largest state after Russia and the sixth-largest in population. Ukrainians and Russians shared the same origins, spoke closely related Slavic languages, and had tightly intertwined histories. Another Slavic people now called Belarusans also shared this history. Their new state of Belarus, due north of Ukraine, was wedged between Russia and Poland. Just to the north of Belarus along the coast of the Baltic Sea were the tiny countries of Lithuania, Latvia, and Estonia. All three had been absorbed by the expanding Russian Empire in the 18th century. They established their independence after World War I, but were occupied and forcibly incorporated into the Soviet Union during World War II. Immediately west of Ukraine was Moldova, an inconspicuous land-locked territory near the Black Sea. It had no history of independence. Its strongest historical and ethnic ties were to Romania.

Further east, on the southern slopes of the Caucasus Mountains, just before Europe ends and Asia begins, were Armenia, Georgia, and Azerbaijan. The Armenians are an ancient nation, the first people in history to make Christianity their state religion. Their history has been a struggle to survive the ambitions of their powerful neighbors. During World War I, more than 1 million Armenians were murdered by the Muslim Ottoman Turks in the first genocide in a century repeatedly scarred by genocidal murder. Georgia, another ancient Christian state located precariously at the edge of the Muslim world, was incorporated into the Russian Empire over several decades, beginning in the 1780s. Georgians reluctantly accepted the Russian takeover as the price of protection from their Muslim neighbors. Azerbaijan, a Turkic-Muslim country with great potential oil wealth, came under Russian rule during the first quarter of the 19th century.

The largest piece of former Soviet territory aside from Russia, and the area about which outsiders knew least, was the region currently known as Central Asia. It consisted of five countries: Kazakhstan, Uzbekistan, Turkmenistan, Kyrgyzstan, and Tajikistan. Unlike Russia and several of the European successor states, none of the Central Asian successor states had ever been an independent nation. Their jagged and convoluted borders dated from the Soviet era and had been drawn to serve the needs of the Soviet Union's Communist dictatorship in Moscow. They were poor—the poorest part of the former Soviet Union—and politically unstable. As parts of the Russian Empire before 1917 and the Soviet Union for seven decades thereafter, they had been treated like colonies: Their natural resources had been exploited and their people had usually been neglected. Like Azerbaijan, the majority of their population was Muslim. Largely ignored by the outside world when they were component parts of the defunct Soviet Union, as independent states they received unprecedented attention, mainly because of their extensive natural resources, particularly oil and natural gas.

In the dozen years that have passed since the states of Central Asia became independent, both their problems and their huge deposits of oil and natural gas have become matters of growing interest and concern to the United States and other major industrial powers. These new countries have all endured economic hardship and social dislocation and have been governed by autocratic regimes. Each is a candidate for serious instability in the future. This book is designed to introduce American young adults to Central Asia, a part of the world that will have a growing impact on their own lives in decades to come.

PART I
History

1
WHAT IS
CENTRAL ASIA?

A vast region far from Eurasia's traditional centers of population and civilization, Central Asia frequently has been a way station, a barrier, or a buffer rather than a primary destination. For more than a thousand years its southern section marked the long and often hazardous middle passage of the Silk Road, the trade route that once connected the Chinese civilization of East Asia with the civilizations of the Mediterranean. Central Asia's deserts and mountains, as well as its physical remoteness, constituted a rugged barrier beyond which great ancient and medieval empires could not expand. For example, in the mid-sixth century B.C., it was the northeastern edge of the Persian Empire; in the first century A.D., it was the northeastern edge of the Parthian Empire. Central Asia also was the northeastern fringe of Alexander the Great's empire in the fourth century B.C. and the distant western outpost of the Chinese Empire during the Tang dynasty in the eighth century A.D. Not until the 13th century, when the fierce Mongol horsemen of Genghis (Chinggis) Khan overran Eurasia, from China to the Middle East and eastern Europe, did all of Central Asia, from its northern grasslands to its southern deserts and mountains, fall to an outside conqueror.

At times, Central Asia has been a buffer zone between peoples and empires. In the 18th century, its northern grasslands separated the Russian and Chinese Empires. In the 19th century, it stood between the expanding Russian and British Empires until the Russians completed their conquest of the region in the 1880s.

Central Asia has been a meeting place, and sometimes a melting pot, for nations and cultures with very different traditions and origins. For millennia nomads of the Eurasian plains met here with the settled inhabitants of the region's river valleys and oases, just as often mingling with them as clashing with them. For several hundred years after the seventh century, Arab-Islamic and Persian cultures fused here. But only rarely were the independent states of Central Asia powerful enough to control the entire region or threaten lands outside its confines. The most notable exception was the short-lived empire of the dreaded conqueror Tamerlane during the late 14th and early 15th centuries. Tamerlane's attacks on countries to the north and west of Central Asia were so destructive that the world outside took note. His ambitious building program turned his capital of Samarkand (today in Uzbekistan) into one of the most beautiful cities of that time. His remarkable grandson, Ulugh Beg, made Samarkand a formidable center of intellectual activity, particularly in the study of astronomy, from the 1420s until the late 1440s.

But Central Asia's main story is of an area through which merchants, travelers, conquerors, and nomadic tribes passed. This was especially true of its northern reaches, the vast grasslands that today are part of Kazakhstan but stretch far beyond its borders into Mongolia and Russia. Long before anyone heard of the Silk Road, these grasslands provided the main route through Eurasia and the main home to loosely organized clans and tribes of nomads. As these nomads moved their herds from pasture to pasture, they transported goods, skills, and traditions between civilizations separated by thousands of uncharted miles. As a rule, only when these nomads—the world's best horsemen and mounted warriors—periodically and suddenly turned from herding to raiding and plundering did sedentary cultures pay serious heed to them or the uncharted vastness from which they came.

Modern Central Asia is an arbitrary political concoction. Geographically it belongs to a larger area (usually called Inner Asia) that extends westward from Kazakhstan and Turkmenistan into China and Mongolia (by some definitions it also extends northward from Kazakhstan and Mongolia into the southern parts of Siberia). In the past, Inner Asia also had a nongeographic name, Turkestan, which referred to the Turkic lan-

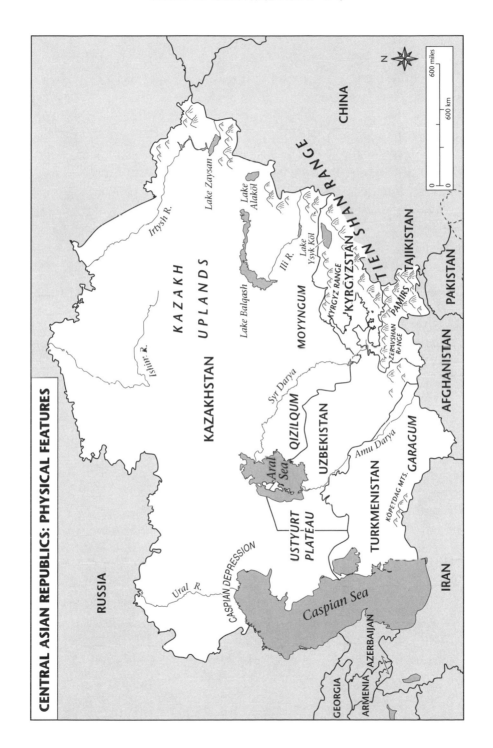

CENTRAL ASIAN REPUBLICS: PHYSICAL FEATURES

RUSSIA

KAZAKHSTAN

KAZAKH UPLANDS

Irtysh R.

Ishim R.

Lake Zaysan

Lake Alaköl

Lake Balqash

Ili R.

Lake Ysyk Köl

MOYYNGUM

KYRGYZ RANGE

KYRGYZSTAN

TIEN SHAN RANGE

CHINA

PAMIRS

TAJIKISTAN

PAKISTAN

AFGHANISTAN

ZERAVSHAN RANGE

Syr Darya

QIZILQUM

UZBEKISTAN

Amu Darya

GARAGUM

KOPETDAG MTS.

TURKMENISTAN

Aral Sea

USTYURT PLATEAU

CASPIAN DEPRESSION

Ural R.

Caspian Sea

IRAN

GEORGIA

ARMENIA AZERBAIJAN

N

600 miles

600 km

guages spoken by the majority of the people who have lived in the region since the Middle Ages. Turkestan, in fact, is a Persian word that means "land of the Turks." More recent political realities led to Turkestan's artificial division into three parts: Mongolia, a vast land wedged between Russia and China; East Turkestan, which became part of China; and West (or Russian) Turkestan, the area that fell under Russia control in the 18th and 19th centuries and became part of the Soviet Union after 1917. Russian Turkestan now is known as Central Asia. It is divided into five independent countries: Kazakhstan, Uzbekistan, Turkmenistan, Kyrgyzstan, and Tajikistan. Kazakhstan alone accounts for two thirds of Central Asia's total area. Uzbekistan and Turkmenistan are each about the size of California. Kyrgyzstan and Tajikistan together account for only 8 percent of the region's territory.

Geography

Central Asia is a huge, jagged trapezoid near the middle of the Eurasian land mass. It covers about 1.5 million square miles (3.9 million square kilometers), which is slightly less than half the area of the continental United States (minus Alaska). It is divided into three main geographic zones: semiarid grasslands in the north, deserts dotted with oases in the south, and snow-capped mountains in the southeast.

About three-quarters of Central Asia's western border, and its main natural frontier, is formed by the Caspian Sea. Although called a sea, it really is a salt lake. With an area of more than 143,000 square miles (370,370 sq km), the Caspian Sea is the world's largest inland body of water, more than four times larger than Lake Superior, its nearest competitor. Over time, both its size and character have changed with the climate. Three million years ago the Caspian was a true sea, much larger than its current size and linked to the oceans of the world via an outlet to the Black Sea. Today, confined to a much smaller shoreline, it is cut off from the open sea. Its surface lies about 100 feet (30.5 m) below sea level, as does the surrounding shoreline (known as the Caspian Depression), the largest (though not the deepest) area of subsea-level land in the world. The Caspian Sea's level has risen and fallen as natural and human-made conditions have varied. In the early 14th century, its surface was about 40 feet (12 m) above its current levels; in the 1840s it was several feet lower. The level of the sea fell by eight feet (2.5 m) between 1929 and 1961 but began rising again after 1978, climbing about eight feet by the end of the mid-1990s before it stabilized. Higher rainfall levels might account for the sea's recent rise, but still scientists cannot fully explain it. About 70 percent of the Caspian's water comes from Europe's longest river, the Volga, whose southern-most section lies just beyond Central Asia's western border. The Caspian Sea, whose waters cover enormous oil and natural gas deposits, also is unbalanced. It reaches a depth of about 3,200 feet (975 m) in the south, but its northern section on average is only 17 feet (5 m) deep. As recently as 10,000 to 8,000 years ago, the northern section of the sea dried up, leaving the Caspian one-third smaller than it is today.

North of the Caspian Sea, an arbitrary line divides Kazakhstan from Russia and marks the rest of Central Asia's western border. The line extends northward just east and parallel to the Volga River for about 250 miles (400 km) before veering sharply to the east and, at the Ural River, crossing from Europe into Asia.

In the south, due eastward from the Caspian Sea, a lowland about 150 miles (240 km) wide rises into a hilly region called the Köpetdag Mountains. These low mountains separate Turkmenistan from northern Iran. Further east are lower-lying deserts where Turkmenistan and Uzbekistan meet Afghanistan. Central Asia's southern tier then climbs steeply until, in Tajikistan and Kyrgyzstan, it reaches the snow-capped Pamirs and the Tien Shan range. Some peaks in these towering mountains rise above 24,000 feet (7,315 m). When the 13th-century Italian traveler Marco Polo crossed these mountains, he called them the Roof of the World. Central Asia's eastern frontier, from south to north, traverses the Tien Shan range in Kyrgyzstan and then, in Kazakhstan, descends to a trackless plain that stretches beyond the horizon in every direction. The region's northern limit is the Kazakhstan-Russian border. On a map, this border makes a wavy, undulating line more than 4,200 miles (6,800 km) long through the emptiness of the Eurasian steppe.

Central Asia is a dry land. Its location near the heart of Eurasia means it does not benefit from the sea breezes that bring the rain and moderate the climates of regions nearer the coast. The Atlantic Ocean to the west and the Pacific Ocean to the east are much too far away to supply moist winds. To the south, the Indian Ocean and its coastal seas—the Arabian

Sea and the Bay of Bengal—are closer, but their winds are blocked by the towering mountain ranges north of the Indian subcontinent. As a result, the vast plains that make up the bulk of the Central Asian landscape are either a semiarid grasslands, known as steppes, or deserts. These plains rise gradually from below sea level at the Caspian Sea's eastern shore to an average elevation of about 1,200 feet (366 m) in eastern Kazakhstan. The grasslands are located in northern Kazakhstan and turn into semi-desert and then desert in the southern part of the country and in Uzbekistan and Turkmenistan.

Central Asia's largest desert region, one of the largest in the world, is bisected by the Amu Darya, one of the region's two main rivers. The Amu Darya carries three times more water than any other river in the region. Formed by tributaries that rise in the Pamirs, the Amu Darya takes a northwestern course toward the Aral Sea. Southwest of the Amu Darya is Turkmenistan's Garagum, or Black Sands desert, where it usually rains about once a decade. To the river's northeast, in Uzbekistan and Kazakhstan, is the Qizilqum, or Red Sands, desert. Together these deserts make up what is called the Turan Lowland. Central Asia's other great river, and its longest (1,680 miles, 1,100 km), the Syr Darya, marks the northern and eastern limits of the Qizilqum. Formed in eastern Uzbekistan by tributaries that rise in the Tien Shan, the Syr Darya generally parallels the Amu Darya as it crosses the desert in Kazakhstan en route toward the Aral Sea.

Because the two rivers provided the essential water in a harsh desert region, Central Asia at one time was called "the land between the rivers." Both rivers once fed the Aral Sea, and were in fact its main source of water. But that changed when the Soviet Union began massive, environmentally reckless irrigation projects in the 1960s. Today only a small and inadequate amount of water from the two rivers (only 10 percent of the former flow) reaches the Aral Sea, which once had the fourth-largest area of any inland body of water in the world. The sea is rapidly drying up. The environmental consequences are nothing short of catastrophic.

The Zeravshan, another major river, descends from the Pamirs in Uzbekistan. It runs between the Syr Darya and the Amu Darya, toward the Amu Darya but then disappears into the sands of the Garagum. Numerous smaller rivers have the same problem: Once they leave the mountains and reach the desert, they receive no tributaries. Evaporation, seepage, and diversion of their waters for irrigation, deplete their flow with every mile. Two Central Asian rivers that complete their journey to a lake or sea are on opposite sides of the region. In the eastern Kazakhstan, the Ili river flows into Lake Balqash, a large but shallow, land-locked lake shaped like a sickle. In the far west, the Ural River reaches the northern end of the Caspian Sea. The only major river in the region to leave Central Asia and reach the open sea is the Irtysh. It flows through eastern Kazakhstan northward into Russia, where it becomes a tributary to the Ob, one of the mighty Siberian rivers that flow into the Arctic Sea.

The arid Central Asian landscape is dotted by many oases. The Amu Darya, Syr Darya, and Central Asia's smaller rivers bring water to the oases that, over the centuries, have become the homes to the region's most important settlements. Most oases are located in arid regions between the mountains and the bone-dry deserts, usually at an altitude of about 1,000 to 1,500 feet (300 to 450 m). Rainfall in these areas is slightly higher than on the hot desert plains, and there is more groundwater. Mary, one of Central Asia's oldest cities (once called Merv), stands on an oasis along the course of the Murgap River in southern Turkmenistan. Tashkent, today the region's largest metropolis, began as an oasis settlement on a tributary of the Syr Darya. Central Asia's major oases were central to the life of the region. Farmers used the precious waters from rivers and underground sources to irrigate farmland and help feed the region, while oasis cities such as Samarkand and Bukhara were trading centers for caravans along the Silk Road and later became important cultural centers as well.

Central Asia's high mountains in the south and east provide an altogether different environment. Rain and snow in the Pamirs and Tien Shan foster both dense forests and lush meadows. For centuries these meadows have provided excellent pastures for nomads to graze their herds of sheep, goats, cattle, and horses. Above the forests and meadows are dozens of glaciers, including the Fedchenko Glacier almost 50 miles (80 km) long, the longest in the entire territory of the former Soviet Union. The Tien Shan and Pamir glaciers cover an area of 6,560 square miles (17,000 sq km) and, along with the annual snow melt, provide vital freshwater for the region.

There are two large basins in these towering mountains. One is the Fergana Valley, a fertile region about 180 miles (290 km) long and 90

miles (145 km) wide at its broadest point, which is the most densely populated part of Central Asia. It lies mainly in Uzbekistan, but small
patches also belong to Kyrgystan and Tajikistan. An irrigation network
built over many generations has turned the Fergana Valley into the
largest oasis in Central Asia. The valley is surrounded by mountains on
the north, east, and south, with a six-mile-wide outlet to the desert region
of Uzbekistan to the west. The second basin, Lake Ysyk Köl, in Kyrgyzstan, is the fourth deepest lake in the world. Lake Ysyk Köl is one of many
glacially fed lakes in the mountains of Kyrgyzstan and Tajikistan.

Climate

Central Asia's lack of rainfall is one feature of its extreme continental climate. Winters are cold. Because of desert air conditions, some regions on
the plains actually are colder than certain lower mountain areas. The
higher elevations in Kyrgyzstan and Tajikistan have bitterly cold winters.
Summers in the Central Asian deserts are insufferably hot. Temperatures in
July often reach 100°F (40°C) in Uzbekistan's major cities (Bukhara,
Samarkand, and Tashkent), as well as in the capital of Turkmenistan (Ashgabat). Even cities in the foothills of the southeastern mountains, such as
Dushanbe (Tajikistan's capital), Bishkek (Kyrgyzstan's capital), and Almaty
(Kazakhstan's former capital), often endure peak summer daytime temper-
atures between 85 and 95°F (30° to 35°C). And the ground is dozens of
degrees hotter than the air. In 1915, the sand temperature in the Garagum
desert in eastern Turkmenistan once reached 174°F. Fortunately, nights are
cool, as temperatures drop quickly after sunset under cloudless desert skies.
This not only brings relief to people but also helps their crops. The cool
summer nights increase the sugar content of melons, grapes, and apricots.
Central Asia's melons seem to have benefited the most. Their reputation
has long extended well beyond Central Asia to Persia and present-day Iraq.
In the past, these were shipped to royalty in special brass cauldrons packed
with ice.

Natural Resources

Central Asia has large deposits of coal, iron, copper, lead, phosphates,
zinc, gold, uranium, and a variety of other minerals. However, by far the

most important natural resources are oil and natural gas, the two essential energy sources that power much of the modern industrialized world. These extremely valuable resources are not equally distributed among the countries of the region, as most of them are beneath or near the Caspian Sea. Kazakhstan has huge deposits of both oil and natural gas, while Turkmenistan has some of the world's largest natural gas deposits and some oil deposits. Uzbekistan has smaller but still significant natural gas deposits. There are very small oil and natural gas deposits in Kyrgyzstan, while Tajikistan must rely on hydroelectric power as its main domestic source of energy.

Environmental Problems

Central Asia is an environmental disaster area, largely as a result of policies followed by the government of the former Soviet Union. The Soviet regime used a region in eastern Kazakhstan as one of its main nuclear test sites, leaving behind radioactive materials that have damaged the health of millions of people over several generations. Nuclear waste dumps along the shore of the Caspian Sea have added to the damage. Industrial pollution from power stations fired by low-grade coal, copper smelters without any pollution controls, and destructive mining practices and other huge factories poisoned people, water, and land. The wastes these enterprises left behind have not been cleaned up and continue to sicken and kill people. Huge areas of farmland were contaminated by DDT and other pesticides and agricultural chemicals. A biological weapons manufacturing complex caused further contamination. Everything was made worse by the enormous irrigation projects that took most of the water from the Amu Darya and Syr Darya and diverted it to gigantic cotton fields, causing the Aral Sea to shrink (see boxed feature on pages 14 and 15). The Aral Sea's slow death has wiped out vegetation and wildlife, worsened the climate, and exposed polluted salt flats to desert winds that spread poisons over tens of thousands of square miles.

Population

More than 100 ethnic groups make up Central Asia's population of about 58 million people. That population is growing at between 1.5 and 2 percent per year, a dangerously high figure for any society but especially serious in a region plagued by economic instability, ethnic strife, and vast governmental corruption. Most of the people in Central Asia are poor—the region was the poorest part of the former Soviet Union—and millions of young people cannot find jobs, a problem that will worsen as more young workers enter the job market each year. The main cultural unifier in Central Asia is Islam. The Sunni version of Islam is the faith of the great majority—probably more than 80 percent—of the population. Two-thirds of the population is also Turkic, meaning they speak one of the languages of the Turkic language family. Neither the religious nor linguistic commonalities have prevented conflict and ethnic strife in Central Asia, either in the past or at the present time.

The Uzbeks, who number about 23 million, are the largest single ethnic group in Central Asia. They are the largest Turkic group outside of Turkey. They are also the largest minority group in Tajikistan, Turkmenistan, and Kyrgyzstan. Their origins may go back as far as the 11th century, but they probably coalesced as an identifiable group a

When this picture was taken in the early 20th century, the Jewish community in Central Asia was about 2,500 years old. Since 1991, most Jews have emigrated from the region. (Courtesy Library of Congress)

hundred or more years before they entered and conquered much of Central Asia in the first decade of the 15th century. The Uzbeks are Sunni Muslims.

Like the Uzbeks, the Kazakhs, who number between 9 million and 10 million, are both a Turkic people and Sunni Muslims. They emerged as a distinct group in the mid-15th century when a number of Uzbek clans broke away from the larger group and settled on Central Asia's steppes. In the 17th century, they divided into three tribal groups before becoming the first Central Asian people to fall under Russian control during the late 18th and 19th centuries.

The third largest ethnic group in Central Asia is neither Turkic nor Muslim nor, for that matter, even Asian. It is Russian (and, to a far lesser extent, Ukrainian). Central Asia's Russians are largely the product of two waves of immigration: the first in the 19th and early 20th centuries, during the days of the Russian Empire, and the second from the 1920s through the 1970s, during the Soviet era. These people are Russian Orthodox Christians and are the largest community of non-Muslims in Central Asia. While precise figures do not exist, at one point in the mid-20th century Russians and Ukrainians together were close to a third of Central Asia's total population. That percentage began to decrease in the 1970s as birthrates among the native peoples exceeded those among the Russians and Ukrainians. The slide grew steeper when Russians and Ukrainians started leaving Central Asia when the Soviet Union began to totter in the late 1980s. It became steeper still as emigration increased after the Soviet Union collapsed in 1991. By 2001, about 7.5 million Russians (and a smattering of Ukrainians) lived in Central Asia, less than 15 percent of the region's population.

Central Asia's fourth-largest ethnic group, the Tajiks, is Muslim but not Turkic. The Tajiks, who have lived in Central Asia since ancient times, speak an Indo-European language closely related to Persian. About 5.5 million Tajiks live in Central Asia, 80 percent in Tajikistan, and the rest in Uzbekistan. Another 6.5 million live in Afghanistan, where they are the country's second-largest ethnic group. During the past 500 years, as Turkic peoples gradually took over most of Central Asia, the Tajiks found themselves increasingly marginalized. This was reflected in the borders drawn during the Soviet era, which deprived the Tajiks of several of their important historical centers.

THE ARAL SEA

Two Central Asian countries, Kazakhstan and Uzbekistan, share the Aral Sea. Until the time of the Soviet Union, the Aral Sea was the center of a productive agricultural area on the deltas of the Amu Darya and Syr Darya rivers. Its clear salty waters supported a vibrant fishing industry. About 160 fishing boats, most sailing from the ports of Muynoq in the south and Aral on its northeastern tip, provided the Soviet Union with about one-sixth of its seafood. Thousands of fishermen caught more than 20 different species of fish. Additional tens of thousands more people earned their living in the fishing industry. The delta region of the Amu Darya and Syr Darya, aside from the crops it produced, also sheltered a wide variety of wildlife, including several species unique to the area. The wetlands of the Amu Darya alone covered well over 1 million acres and contained dozens of lakes. A nature reserve on an island in the middle of the sea protected a number of rare animals. Beautiful and pristine beaches lined the Aral's shore.

All of that changed when the Soviet government began diverting the waters of the Amu Darya and Syr Darya to irrigate enormous new cotton fields. The Soviet Union wanted to become an exporter of cotton because it was a valuable cash crop. The Soviet economic planners called it "white gold." The irrigation was done with a series of canals, the largest of which was the Garagum, a canal almost 900 miles (1,450 km) long stretching across the desert of Turkmenistan. One expert described it as "a leech sucking the lifeblood from the beneficial [Amu Darya] river." It was an apt description. Not only did the Garagum and other canals take 90 percent of the water from the two rivers, they were so poorly planned and constructed that half of the water was wasted. Meanwhile, the cotton fields were doused and saturated with tons of pesticides, fertilizers, and herbicides that protected the cotton but were toxic to animals, plants, and people.

The diversion of water began in 1959, and by the early 1980s the Soviet Union indeed was the world's second-largest exporter of cotton, but only at a horrendous price. Starved of its water, the Aral Sea began to dry up. Change came quickly. In 1950 the southern port of Muynoq was on an island in the Amu Darya delta. By 1962 the island was a crooked peninsula, and by 1970 Muynoq was high and dry, surrounded by newly exposed desert, six miles from a shoreline becoming more distant each day. By the 1980s the sea was 25 miles away, and by 1990 more than 40 miles. The situation was the same in the north. In 1994 a Western journalist described the scene from the former fishing town of Aral:

> Where Aral waters once lapped, naked seabeds gleamed with salts. . . . The sea was so far away now that to view its remains I needed an aircraft . . . I was aloft over what had been a rich oasis. . . . Beneath me was only a salt pan. Finally we reached the water, but not the sea. Shrunken to half its former size, the Aral has divided into two shallow bodies—briny lakes in a platter of caustic marzipan.

By the mid-1990s the Aral Sea had lost more than half its area and about two-thirds of its volume. Its water level had dropped by 44 feet (13.5 m). The water that was left, almost three times as salty as before, was uninhabitable for most species of fish. There were now, in fact, two Aral Seas: a smaller northern sea and a larger, oddly shaped southern sea. The bountiful wetlands of the Amu Darya delta had practically vanished, reduced to less than one-twentieth of their former size. More than half the species of mammals were gone, and almost half the species of birds. The fishing industry was dead, the exposed former seabed littered with the hulks of beached boats that once had trolled for fish or transported goods across the sea. Winds sweeping over the exposed seabed picked up tons of salt and toxic chemical residues and deposited them on the surrounding countryside, ruining farmland and damaging the health of millions of people. Rates of cancer, tuberculosis, bronchitis, typhoid, and other serious diseases soared, as did the rate of maternal death in childbirth and infant mortality. The deserts in the region around the dying sea were expanding at the frightening rate of about two million acres per year, a pace exceeded only by the expansion of the Sahara in Africa.

The list goes on. After independence, the governments of Uzbekistan and Kazakhstan had neither the resources nor the will to deal with the environmental crisis. In 1993 the five Central Asian states signed an agreement to establish a fund for restoration efforts. In recent years, several international organizations ranging from the World Bank to the European Union have become involved in efforts to find a solution to this environmental catastrophe. Restoring the sea even slightly will require massive investments. The irrigation system must be improved and the size of the water-hungry cotton fields must be cut drastically. No matter what is done, much of the damage is beyond repair.

The two least numerous of Central Asia's major Turkic peoples are the Turkmen (Turkomans) and the Kyrgyz. Both groups are Sunni Muslims. The Turkmen of today, who number about 3.6 million in Central Asia and about 1.5 million more in Iran and Afghanistan, are descended from nomadic tribes that during the Middle Ages lived in Mongolia. Between the 14th and 16th centuries they seem to have coalesced as the ethnic group that exists today. The Kyrgyz are thought to have originated in eastern Siberia and migrated over several centuries as tribal groups into Central Asia to their current mountain home. Closely related to the Kazakhs, they number about 3 million and became a distinct people in the 16th century.

Smaller communities with diverse origins and backgrounds also are scattered across the region, including ethnic Germans and Koreans who were deported there by the Soviet government during World War II; Muslim Tartars, who settled in the region in the mid-19th century; Pashtuns, the largest ethnic group in Afghanistan; and Uighurs, who form the majority of northwest China (the former East Turkestan). One group that has almost disappeared in the past 10 years but which has an ancient history in Central Asia is the Jewish community. It is believed that the first Jews arrived more than 2,500 years ago, when the Babylonians conquered their homeland in what today is Israel and exiled many of their ancestors. The community survived ups and downs over more than two millennia, including seven decades of Soviet hostility toward religion. Since the collapse of the Soviet Union, fear of Islamic extremism and economic hard times have led most of Central Asia's Jews to emigrate, mainly to Israel and the United States. Of a Jewish community that numbered more than 200,000 in 1991, only a few thousand, many of them older people, are left in Central Asia today.

NOTES

p. 14 " 'a 'leech sucking the lifeblood . . .'" Svat Soucek, A History of Inner Asia (Cambridge, England: Cambridge University Press, 2000), p. 8.

p. 15 " 'Where Aral waters once lapped, . . .' " Mike Edwards, "Soviet Pollution," National Geographic, August 1994, p. 91.

2

ANCIENT TIMES TO THE 19TH CENTURY

Central Asia's recorded history begins about 2,500 years ago. At that time the people who occupied most of the region were nomads, although some soon settled down, built irrigation systems along the rivers, and founded the region's oldest towns and cities. These early inhabitants spoke dialects closely related to modern-day Persian, the language spoken today in Iran. Persian belongs to the Iranian subgroup of the Indo-European language family—the language family that includes English and most other languages spoken in Europe.* Part of the legacy of Central Asia's first known settlers is the names of places they left behind after they were lost to history. Many of the region's oldest towns, such as Samarkand and Tashkent, have names that end in -kand, -kent, or -kat, all of which are variations of the Iranian word for town. The word *darya* (or *dar'ya*), which is part of the name of both of Central Asia's two main rivers, the Amu Darya and the Syr Darya, is the Iranian word for lake or sea. Today the name of every country in the region (Kazakhstan, Uzbekistan, etc.) ends with the syllable -*stan*, an Iranian word that means "place," "tent," "abode," or "camp." It has the same origins as the English verb *to stand*.

The best remembered of these ancient Iranian-speaking groups probably are the Scythians, legendary horsemen and warriors of the steppe in

---

*For the sake of simplicity and clarity, the terms *Persian* and *Iranian* will be used interchangeably in this text.

both Asia and Europe who also created magnificent gold and silver decorative art. For centuries the Scythians wandered across the northern steppe of Central Asia and beyond, toward both the east and west. In about 700 B.C., some Scythian tribes moved westward into Europe, where they took control of the plains north of the Black Sea in what today is Ukraine and southern Russia. They held sway there for about 400 years. Scythians are best known for their exploits in Europe. But the tribes living on the plains north of the Syr Darya played a significant role in the early history of Central Asia before they disappeared more than two millennia ago.

The first major state to have any influence in Central Asia was the ancient Persian Empire, a huge empire that extended from the Balkans and North Africa in the west to India in the east. At its peak around 500 B.C., it controlled most of the territory between the Amu Darya and Syr Darya. The most common ancient name for that region was Transoxiana—that is, the area beyond, or north of, the river Oxus, the Greek name for the Amu Darya. The Persians, whose Central Asian dominions extended almost to the Aral Sea, created the largest and most powerful empire of the ancient world, until they met their match and were conquered by the Greek king Alexander the Great in 329 B.C. Alexander was one of history's greatest conquerors and the greatest general of his time. After defeating the Persians and seizing most of their empire, Alexander pushed into Central Asia as he headed toward India, his ultimate goal. There he met strong resistance from local rulers before he conquered territory as far north as the Syr Darya. Among the cities he conquered was Samarkand, at the time already an important trading town center and the center of an Iranian-speaking kingdom called Sogdiana.

Alexander encountered the most stubborn resistance he had yet faced from the Scythians. Two centuries earlier they had fought the mighty Persians to a standstill on the eastern European steppe north of the Black Sea. Now the Scythians destroyed the first army Alexander sent against them in Central Asia. Although Alexander eventually managed to defeat the Scythians, his energy, and that of his army, was spent. He left Central Asia and died in the Middle Eastern city of Babylon in 323 B.C. His enormous but unwieldy empire, which stretched from Greece to India, soon broke up. Interestingly, although Alexander was an invader from outside the region, he was widely admired and even today is considered something of a folk hero in many parts of Central Asia.

After Alexander's empire broke up, part of southern Central Asia remained under the control of one of its Greek-ruled successor states, the Seleucid kingdom. That control lasted only about 70 years. In the mid-third century B.C., the Seleucids were driven from Central Asia by the Persian-speaking Parthians. The former Seleucid territories in the region at first were divided between the Parthian Empire in the west and another Greek-ruled state, the Bactrian Empire, in the east. The Parthians were a nomadic people from the lowlands east of the Caspian Sea who probably were closely related to the Scythians. They established a powerful state, most of whose territory actually lay outside Central Asia. However, the Parthians also eventually won control of a slice of Central Asia well south of the Aral Sea and east of the Caspian Sea, seizing Bactrian territory as they expanded eastward. Their capital, Nisa, was in southern Turkmenistan, about six miles west of the current capital of Ashgabat. In its glory days under the Parthians, Nisa's royal palace was surrounded by a wall with 43 towers, and the city itself was a thriving commercial center. Nisa actually outlasted the Parthian Empire (which endured until the mid-third century A.D.) by a thousand years, surviving until the invading Mongols burnt it to the ground in the 13th century. It was one of a number of Central Asian cities that never recovered from destruction by the Mongols. Today its weathered ruins lie on a grassy plateau in the foothills of the Körpetdag Mountains.

In the second half of the second century B.C., a new group of nomadic invaders from the Eurasian steppe upset the balance of power in Central Asia. While the Parthian Empire survived the storm from the northeast, the invaders destroyed the Bactrian Empire. The newcomers, driven from their homeland by other nomads, were an Indo-European group who soon adopted the Iranian language of the people they conquered. Around the time of Christ, they established a powerful new state, the Kushan Empire. Except for some Parthian territory in what today is Turkmenistan, it controlled all of Central Asia south of the Aral Sea. However, the core of the new empire lay outside Central Asia. At its peak in the late first and early second centuries, it extended into India and as far south as the Arabian Sea.

Both the Kushan and Parthian Empires benefited from the Silk Road, the first steady trade route between China and the Mediterranean world, which began to operate in the late first century B.C. The Silk Road was not a single highway, but several alternate caravan paths through the deserts and mountains of inner Asia. It crossed Central Asia along two routes, southern and northern, enriching the cities and towns, as well as the organized states to which they belonged, along the way. These two routes met just northeast of the city of Merv (now called Mary). There the Silk Road tracked to the southwest before crossing into Persia. The Silk Road also brought the Buddhist religion to Central Asia, a faith that became the religion of the ruling dynasty of the Kushan Empire.

Both the Parthian and Kushan Empires collapsed in the third century. The Parthians fell first, to a revived Persian Empire under the Sassanid dynasty. The Persians then destroyed the Kushan Empire to their east, ending up with control of most of Central Asia south of the Aral Sea, as well as vast territories from the Middle East to India. This seemed to restore the state of affairs that had existed 800 years earlier during the time of the original Persian Empire. The Sassanids, in fact, would rule a powerful Persian state for about 400 years. Then new invaders from the south arrived and brought permanent change to Central Asia in the form of a new religion. It was one of two fundamental changes—the other involving population—on the horizon. Over time these two changes would remake the region.

The Coming of Islam

Until the seventh century, no single religion dominated Central Asia. Rather, a variety of faiths coexisted in the region. The most ancient religions were the indigenous shamanistic cults of the nomads, which had followers all across Eurasia. The oldest of the more formal and organized religions in Central Asia prior to the seventh century, as well as the one with the largest following, was Zoroastrianism, the indigenous religion of Persia. Zoroastrianism was a dualistic religion—that is, it posited an eternal struggle between the forces of good and evil—with roots in Persia that stretched back to the sixth century B.C. Its status as the official religion of the Sassanid dynasty gave it an advantage in winning followers in areas under the Persian Empire's control. Buddhism had a small regional following but also relatively deep roots, having reached Central Asia via the Silk Road at about the same time as Zoroastrianism. Manichaeism, another dualistic religion, was founded in the third century in what today is Iraq. It had a small following north of the Amu Darya. It combined elements from Christianity, Zoroastrianism, and religious influences from India. Christianity, in particular the Nestorian church, also had established itself in Central Asia, especially around the city of Merv. There also were Jewish communities in the region.

Islam in the seventh century was a very young religion. Its founder, a merchant named Muhammad, began preaching to fellow Arabs of the Arabian Peninsula about A.D. 610. From the start, warfare and conquest played a central role in Islam's spread. By the time of Muhammad's death in 632, his armies had conquered the entire peninsula, from which all Jews and Christians were expelled eight years later. Following the example of Muhammad, his Arab followers began a campaign of conquest, called jihad, or holy war, to spread their religion beyond their homeland to the entire world. The speed and scope of their conquests, which often caused enormous destruction and suffering, was spectacular. Within 100 years the Arabs had conquered an area stretching from Spain in the west to northern India in the east. The Persian Empire was overrun in the 640s and the last Persian emperor killed in 651, having made his final, futile stand against the Arabs at Merv. Although the Arabs had entered Central Asia in triumph, opposition stiffened as they tried to push deeper into the region. Their advance over the next several decades was slow, especially in mountainous regions. Still, that advance did not stop, in part because of divisions between the various groups in Central Asia and a lack of good local leadership. Arab armies reached Bukhara in 709 and Samarkand in 712. The Arabs immediately built mosques in both cities and deported much of the native population to make room for themselves. The conquest often took a historic as well as a human toll. Thus in 712, Arab armies put down a rebellion in a region south of the Aral Sea along the Silk Road in present-day Uzbekistan, a reconquest "which included the slaughter of most of the upper classes and destruction of much of the cultural heritage of the province."

Three years later the Arabs took Tashkent and occupied the Fergana Valley. Resistance then again stiffened, forcing Arab forces to retreat from some of the territory they had conquered. The Arabs provoked a general revolt in Transoxiana in 728 when they attempted to suppress local religions and convert the entire local population to Islam. The revolt was put down after several years of fighting, setting the stage for the decisive battle for control of Central Asia.

THE BATTLE OF TALAS AND ITS AFTERMATH

That battle would not be fought by Central Asians, but rather between two outside powers, the Arabs and the Chinese. Between about 200 B.C. and A.D. 200, the Chinese Empire under the Han dynasty had extended its control almost to the eastern fringes of Central Asia, an effort that promoted trade and the beginning of the Silk Road. The collapse of the Han dynasty removed the Chinese from the region for 500 years. By the eighth century, the Chinese, resurgent under the vigorous Tang dynasty, attempted to push their influence farther west than ever before. This time, however, they were not the only powerful invaders in the region. As the Chinese were pushing west, Arab armies were moving east. At this point, the Chinese, usually skilled in diplomacy, blundered. They executed the Turkic leader who controlled Tashkent and then sacked the city. This act turned the local people against the Chinese and gave the Arabs welcome allies. When the Chinese and Arab armies finally met in July 751 at the Talas River, in what today is northern Kazakhstan, the Arab forces and their allies crushed the Chinese, permanently driving them from Central Asia. The outcome of the battle was reinforced by other long-term developments. Far behind the front lines, the Islamic Arab state based in Baghdad, known as the Abbasid Caliphate, was gaining strength, while the Tang dynasty in China was beginning to weaken. The Arabs and their Islamic converts were militant and often fanatical in their determination to spread their religion. The more tolerant Chinese lacked such ambition. As a result, although the Arabs themselves soon would have to retreat from Central Asia, their victory at the Battle of Talas and the vigor of the Abbasid dynasty were decisive. They pulled Central Asia into the orbit of Islam, where it has remained to this day.

The Arabs gained an unexpected bonus from their victory at Talas, one that eventually would bring incalculable benefits to the Islamic world and then to Christian Europe. Among the prisoners taken at Talas were Chinese experts in the manufacture of paper. According to legend, paper was invented in China by a court official in the first century, but in fact it probably was invented two centuries earlier. It was much better suited for printing and writing and far cheaper to produce than papyrus or parchment, the materials used in the Middle East and Mediterranean world. The Arabs soon learned how to make paper from their captives. It was being manufactured in Samarkand before the end of 751, in Baghdad by 794, and in Egypt by 810. Papermaking reached Europe when it was introduced in Spain about 1150, and from there it spread to France, Italy, Germany, and the rest of Europe. It played a crucial role in disseminating knowledge throughout the Islamic world, and then in the intellectual and economic progress in Europe that eventually contributed so much to the birth of the modern world in the West.

Central Asia's Persian/Muslim Civilization

The Arabs of the Abbasid Caliphate only ruled Central Asia for a short time, during the eighth and part of the ninth centuries. During that period the Arabs suppressed Zoroastrianism and Islam took firm root. Central Asian culture became a fusion of Persian and Islamic traditions in which cultural and intellectual activities flowered, and Arabic became the region's language of government, literature, commerce, and science. This process of cultural development and fusion did not stop when the Abbasid Caliphate weakened in the ninth century. The Persian Samanid dynasty, which took over from the Arabs, encouraged the development of Persian culture and promoted Islam. Their capital, Bukhara, became one of the Islamic world's leading centers of culture and learning, famous for its seminaries and its scholars, scientists, poets, and writers. One 11th-century poet described the city as "the home of glory. . . . the place of assembly of all eminent people of the age." By then Persian had reclaimed its former role as the language of the educated elite, and as the language of culture and science. Along with Bukhara, Samarkand stood out as a center of Islamic-Persian culture.

The outstanding representative of this cultural fusion was Avicenna (980–1037), a Persian born near Bukhara in present-day Uzbekistan whose

Avicenna (Ibn Sina) is probably best known for his medical encyclopedia. More than 1 million words long, it was being used as a textbook in some parts of the West more than 500 years after it was written. (Courtesy Free Library of Philadelphia)

Arabic name was Ibn Sina. Educated in Bukhara, Avicenna studied philosophy and became a renowned physician. His medical encyclopedia, *Canons of Medicine*, was one of the pioneering works of its time. It discussed, for example, how contaminated water supplies could spread certain diseases. The book also codified the medical thought of the ancient Greeks and Romans and listed 760 pharmaceutical drugs. After being translated into Latin, the *Canons of Medicine* achieved recognition beyond the Islamic world as a basic medical text at universities in medieval Europe. Avicenna also was one of the leading medieval Islamic philosophers. His main philosophical work, the *Book of Healing*, drew on the ancient Greek philosophers Aristotle and Plato as well as on Islamic sources to discuss the nature of God and the human soul.

Another remarkable Central Asian scholar was al-Biruni (973–1048), a scientist, poet, and historian who is best known for his work in astronomy and applied mathematics. An ethnic Persian like Avicenna, al-Biruni was born near the present-day city of Khiva in Turkmenistan. He wrote literally dozens of books on topics ranging from the movement of planets, the Moon, and the Sun to a social and geographic study of India, where he traveled for many years, as well as a book on the properties of precious stones. These and other books were remarkably well informed and made al-Biruni one of the most distinguished scientists of his time anywhere in the world.

The Coming of the Turks

When the Arabs brought Islam to Central Asia, the region was inhabited primarily by people who spoke Persian (and therefore Indo-European) languages, as it had been for more than 1,000 years. Some of those Persian speakers were nomads who arrived in the region at different times, while others were settled in one place, on farms or in towns and cities. This division between nomads and settled people would not change for many centuries. What did eventually change was the identity of the nomads moving into Central Asia. As early as the fourth century, nomads speaking Turkic languages, whose original homelands were in eastern Siberia and Mongolia, began pushing into the steppes of northern Central Asia. The first group to arrive were the warlike Huns, who in the fourth and fifth centuries overran large parts of the Sassanid empire. These assaults took place while other Huns were rampaging across Europe and attacking the weakening Roman Empire. New invasions followed. Over a period of centuries, the invasions grew into an unstoppable Turkic tide. At first, the change in population from Indo-European to Turkic took place only in the north (today, Kazakhstan), which became a predominantly Turkic region by the sixth century. The rest of Central Asia, with its much larger population concentrated in the river valleys and oases, remained predominantly Persian-speaking for hundreds of years, until approximately the 13th century.

The ethnic identity of Central Asia's rulers, however, underwent a permanent change well before that. In the tenth century, Samanid rule was overthrown by Turkic invaders from the north. When the smoke cleared, Central Asia was divided between two rival Turkic dynasties that spent much of their time attacking each other's territory. Both dynasties were destroyed in the 11th century by new Turkic invaders, the Seljuks, whose conquests included Persia and large parts of the Middle East farther to the west. Seljuk power in Central Asia waned within a century, as new Turkic invaders continued to pour into Central Asia and carve up the region into short-lived new states.

Meanwhile, the Turkic languages of the new invaders were being fused into the cultural mix of Central Asia. These new languages gradually came to be spoken by the most of the population in Transoxiana. At the same time, Persian, which in recent centuries had made a comeback and displaced Arabic, remained the primary language of the region's educated elite. In fact, in the centuries that followed the first Turkic invasions, the process of cultural influence worked both ways: The region's new Turkic rulers imposed their language on most of the people in the region, and at the same time, they accepted Islam, adopted Persian and many elements of Persian culture, and became bilingual. Once this cultural mixture evolved, it remained in place until the 19th century.

The Mongol Conquest and Its Consequences

Until the early 13th century, the Mongols were disunited nomadic tribes living on the east Asian steppe north of China's Great Wall. They spoke a language distantly related to the Turkic languages already spreading through Central Asia. Skilled mounted warriors, the Mongols traditionally spent much of their time in combat with each other. This changed early in the 13th century when a chieftain named Genghis (Chinggis) Khan succeeding in uniting the tribes. He then forged them into a military machine unmatched up to that time. It was a ruthless and efficient fighting force that conquered Eurasia from China and Korea to eastern Europe and the Middle East. The Mongols created the largest land empire the world had ever seen.

The Mongol conquest of Central Asia took place between 1219 and 1223 and brought catastrophic destruction to the region. Entire cities were destroyed, their populations massacred, their vital irrigation works smashed. Terror was an integral part of Mongol military tactics: cities were torched and their people killed as examples to others. Others who got news of these atrocities often surrendered without a fight. Bukhara was sacked and burned to the ground. Thirty thousand people were killed in the fighting, but afterward most of its population was allowed to live. To the survivors, and the rest of the people of Central Asia, Genghis Khan delivered a message, appropriately while standing in front of a huge pile of heads: "You ask who I am, who speaks this to you. Know, then, that I am the scourge of God." In Samarkand, thousands of inhabitants were massacred after the city fell. Skilled craftsmen were spared, only to be deported to Mongolia, another common Mongol practice. An even worse fate befell Urgench, a city near the Amu Darya delta. When its citizens put up strong resistance, the Mongols broke a dam on the river above the city and flooded it. They then killed the entire population except for some craftsmen. In Merv, only about 400 people, all craftsmen, survived. They were deported to Mongolia. Some cities, especially where the Mongols destroyed irrigation systems, never were rebuilt. Others, such as Merv, a city that in pre-Mongol times was praised for its fine libraries and called the "Pearl of the East," reemerged from the rubble only as shadows of their former selves. In the region immediately south of Lake Balqash, all agricultural and urban life disappeared completely, largely because Mongols chose to live there and use the local grasslands as pasture for their herds. More than a century later, a contemporary geographer described that area:

A person who has traveled in the provinces of Turkestan and passed through its villages told me that only scattered traces and collapsed ruins have remained; the traveler sees from afar what appears like a village with solid buildings and green surroundings, and he looks forward to finding friendly inhabitants, but upon reaching it, he finds the building still standing but devoid of humans except for some nomads and herders, without any agriculture, for what is green there consists of grass as the Creator has let it grow, with steppe vegetation which nobody has sown or planted.

Not until the area fell under Russian rule in the 1860s did the region south of Lake Balqash again support farms and towns.

The Mongols did not come to Central Asia alone. The bulk of their armies were made up of Turkic soldiers whose tribes had been swept up by and made part of the Mongol advance across Eurasia. As these soldiers and additional new waves of arrivals from the steppe settled in Central Asia, they quickened the pace at which the region's population was becoming Turkic rather than Iranian. The destruction of many Persian cities and centers of learning reinforced this process. Iranians increasingly became a minority in a region they had dominated for at least 1,500 years. The newly arrived Turkic people increasingly became the majority. This ethnic transformation, following the religious one of Islamization, was a second major turning point in the history of Central Asia.

There was a recovery once the new Mongol order was established. That order was maintained after Genghis Khan's death, even as his empire was divided among his four sons. Bukhara, Samarkand, and, amazingly, Urgench were among the cities that came back. Samarkand became the busiest commercial center and most important city in the region. The Mongols reestablished security along the Silk Road that had not existed for some time, which revived trade and brought some prosperity to the region. Not only merchants but also travelers with other interests journeyed along the Silk Road, including Marco Polo, whose book about the wonders of the East caused a sensation in Europe. However, by the 14th century Mongol power was on the wane, opening the door for a new empire.

The Empire of Tamerlane

The man who built the new empire was Tamerlane, the son of the chieftain of a minor Turkic clan near Samarkand who could claim descent from Genghis Khan. Tamerlane was a worthy descendent, both as a brilliant general and ruthless conqueror whose military exploits were matched only by his cruelty and egomania. Tamerlane began his career by winning a struggle for control of Central Asia. He went on a campaign of conquest that took him from northern India in the east to modern-day Iran, Iraq, Syria, Turkey, and the plains of Ukraine and southern Russia in the west. He murdered and plundered on a staggering scale wherever he went, and, following Genghis Khan's example, forcibly brought thousands of artisans and craftsmen to his capital city of Samarkand. The city was rebuilt on a grand and lavish scale. Tamerlane also brought scholars to Samarkand, and they made the city a cultural and intellectual center. All of this was done to realize the conqueror's vision of making Samarkand the urban center of the entire world. His empire was the most powerful ever to be based in Central Asia. It extended east to west from northern India to the eastern edges of Anatolia and the Black Sea, and south to north from the Arabian Sea to the southern tip of the Aral Sea. But it did not last long. Tamerlane died in 1405, having just set out to conquer China. His empire split in half

Tamerlane's tomb in Samarkand also is the final resting place for two of his sons and grandsons, including Ulugh Beg. (Courtesy Free Library of Philadelphia)

almost immediately, although its eastern half, which included Central Asia, was ruled by his son and then his grandson for another four decades. After that, the empire crumbled and Central Asia became a patchwork of small states.

Tamerlane's cultural legacy was more impressive than his political one. The scholars he brought to Central Asia and the support he gave them initiated a regional flowering of Islamic civilization. It took the form of a revival of Persian art and architecture and the emergence, for the first time, of a Turkic dialect (Chagatai) as a literary language. The cultural renaissance reached its pinnacle under Ulugh Beg, Tamerlane's grandson, who ruled in Samarkand from 1409 to 1449. Ulugh Beg was a generous patron of art and literature, and he constructed many beautiful public buildings. He also built three *madrasas*, or Islamic schools, in Central Asia, including one each in Samarkand and Bukhara. They were most unusual. While Islamic *madrasas* usually focused on theology and training clerics, Ulugh Beg's schools also emphasized science. His school in Samarkand became a famous center for astronomy and mathematics, and the state-of-the-art astronomical observatory he built there attracted scientists from all over the world. But time was running out. Ulugh Beg was murdered in 1449, ending the remarkable cultural era in Central Asia.

Uzbeks and Kazakhs

The next rulers of Central Asia were tribes that collectively became known as the Uzbeks. They arrived as nomads but soon settled down in the main towns of Transoxiana and began assimilating with the native population. At first, a single state controlled the region, but it was undermined by several factors, include the erosion of its economic base. For centuries the oases of Central Asia had depended on revenues from trade along the Silk Road. But by 1500, the Europeans who were the main customers for goods that reached the western terminus of the Silk Road had found a new, faster, and cheaper route to East Asia: the sea route around the southern tip of Africa. The Silk Road became obsolete. Central Asia sank into economic decline and increasing isolation. By the 17th century three Uzbek states under rulers with absolute power—known either as khans or emirs—controlled parts of southern Central Asia; the khanate of Kokand, centered in the Fergana Valley; the emirate of Bukhara, whose core was in the Zeravshan Valley; and the khanate of Khiva, located in the west along the Amu Darya. They constantly conspired and fought against each other, succeeding mainly in inflicting damage on their rivals and shifting borders back and forth rather than building any enduring strength. Meanwhile, without commercial activity along the Silk Road, Samarkand, Bukhara, and other major cities in the region slipped into decline. None of these entities was a national state. Rather, they were made up of ruling dynasties that controlled territories occupied by a hodgepodge of ethnic groups, some sedentary and some nomad, few of which felt any loyalty to those dynasties or their territorial claims.

Constant raids by nomads from the northern steppe made matters worse. By the 16th century these nomads were the Kazakhs, who were the descendants of Uzbek clans that had set off on their own in the mid-15th century. They eventually divided into three groups known as *hordes*, a word derived from the Turkish word meaning "camp" or "tent." The Great Horde controlled what today is eastern and southern Kazakhstan. The Middle Horde controlled the north-central part of the country, and the Lesser Horde controlled the west. During the 17th and 18th centuries they all faced attacks by powerful nomads called Kalmyks, who originally came from Mongolia. Meanwhile, the Kazakhs were the first Central Asians to confront a new outside power moving toward them from the west: the Russian Empire. Beginning in the 1730s and 1740s, the Kazakhs of the Lesser and Middle Hordes sought Russian protection against the Kalmyks. Russian protection eventually turned into Russian control before the end of the 18th century. The Greater Horde met a similar fate during the 1820s. A new era in Central Asia was about to begin. It would bring the region face to face with powerful forces associated with the modern world and eventually impose painful change to societies set in their traditional ways.

NOTES

p. 21 "which included the slaughter of . . ." Svat Soucek, *A History of Inner Asia* (Cambridge, England: Cambridge University Press, 2000), p. 59.

p. 23 "'the home of glory . . .'" Quoted in Edgar Knobloch, *Monuments of Central Asia: A Guide to the Archaeology, Art and Architecture of Turkestan* (London and New York: I. B. Tauris Publishers, 2001), p. 65.

p. 27 "'You ask who I am . . .'" Quoted in Ahmed Rashid, *Jihad: The Rise of Militant Islam in Central Asia* (New Haven, Conn.: Yale University Press, 2002), p. 23.

p. 27 "'A person who has traveled in the provinces . . .'" Quoted in Soucek, *A History of Inner Asia,* p. 115.

3

RUSSIAN CENTRAL ASIA

At dawn on June 15, 1865, an Orthodox priest armed only with a cross held high above his head led Russian soldiers through the gates of the walled city of Tashkent. Two days of bloody fighting followed before the city surrendered. It had been a lopsided battle that illustrated the growing discrepancy between the power of technologically advanced European states, even semi-modern European states such as Russia, and the premodern states of Asia. At Tashkent, 2,000 Russian soldiers had defeated a native army of more than 30,000. Both the winning and losing sides in the battle seemed to understand that a turning point in the history of the region had taken place. While the Russians had been encroaching on Central Asia for more than a century and had taken a number of small towns, Tashkent was the first major city to fall into their hands. With a population of about 100,000, it was the largest city in Central Asia. All of this may explain why General Mikhail G. Chernyayev, the Russian officer whose troops took the city, was recognized for his achievement both by the country he served and the people he had fought. From his emperor, the czar of Russia, the general received a diamond-encrusted sword. From the defeated defenders, perhaps in an attempt to convince themselves that they could have lost their prized city only to a great conqueror, he received an unofficial but imposing title: the Lion of Tashkent.

The 16th-century Kukeldash Madrasa, pictured here in 1872, was one of the few old Tashkent buildings to survive the disastrous earthquake that hit the city in 1966. (Courtesy Library of Congress)

The Russians Come to Central Asia

Contact between the people of Russia and the people of Central Asia, in peaceful trade and in war, dates back more than a thousand years. The modern period in that long story dates from the early 17th century when the expanding Russian Empire pushed across the Siberian plain to the shores of the Pacific Ocean. While some Russians were pushing east, others turned south, either as traders or raiders. Their presence, while making only a minor impact, turned out to be a sign of things to come. In the early 18th century, several military expeditions sent by Czar Peter the Great failed to establish a permanent Russian presence on the eastern shore of the Caspian Sea and the northern steppes of present-day Kazakhstan. However, they did succeed in building and defending a fort on the steppe at the mouth of the Om River, today the city of Omsk, just north of the current Russian-Kazakh border. In effect, they had built the first forward base for the coming assault on Central Asia. In 1718, the

Russians built another fort called Semipalatinsk in what today is northeastern Kazakhstan. Its lasting importance, it turned out, lay three and a half centuries in the future. In the second half of the 20th century, Semipalatinsk would become notorious as the place where the Soviet Union conducted hundreds of nuclear tests. Their poisonous legacy—horrendous health problems and environmental pollution—has outlasted Russian-Soviet rule and will continue to cause harm in the future.

By the end of the 18th century, the Russians controlled most of the Kazakh steppe. They maintained that control despite a series of revolts during the first three decades of the 19th century. The most serious broke out in 1838 and was not completely suppressed until 1845. The key issue was grazing land, which the Russians had progressively taken from the Kazakhs to the point where they did not have enough pasture on which to graze their herds. The rebellion was led by Kenisary Qasimov, a charismatic figure from a prominent family in the Middle Horde. Kenisary was a skilled warrior who eventually attracted more than 20,000 fighters to his cause. It turned out to be something of a last stand: the last time the Kazakh Middle Horde acted together as a united group. Kenisary's exploits against the Russians, even though they ended in defeat, made him the subject of many poems and songs in the years immediately after

This was the way a bazaar looked in Semipalatinsk circa 1885, during the lifetime of Kazakh writer Abay Kunanbayev. In 1949 the Soviet regime established its main nuclear test site about 100 miles southwest of the city. (Courtesy Library of Congress)

his death. Kenisary also was something of a visionary who lamented both his people's lack of unity and the threats they faced from fellow Central Asians as well as Russians. His ability to see things in historical perspective is one reason many Kazakhs today consider him to be the first Kazakh nationalist. While fighting the Russians, Kenisary used poetry to describe the two-pronged dilemma his people faced:

> The Russians come from the North,
> Kokand from the South.
> Having established fortifications, they trample us.
> From whom would we have both this squeezing
> and this crowding
> We the children of the Kazakhs,
> What would be if we had unity?
> Until now we have been split
> Because we have no unity.

After his own movement was defeated, Kenisary, having accepted amnesty from the Russians, joined a Kyrgyz rebellion against Kokand, the Central Asian power he considered a threat to his people. He was killed in battle during that war in 1847. The Russians meanwhile responded to Kenisary's rebellion by strengthening their own military forces on the steppe and quickening the pace of Russian settlement there. This enabled them to more easily suppress two more Kazakh rebellions during the 1850s and end once and for all organized Kazakh opposition to their control of the steppe region.

By the 19th century, the Russians were eyeing the southern part of Central Asia. Nineteenth-century Russian expansion southward in Central Asia was driven by a variety of motivations. The primary ones probably were economic. There were the profitable trade opportunities with the states in the south, which by the early 19th century were recovering from earlier economic and political setbacks. More important, by the middle of the century the Russians wanted land on which they could grow cotton to supply the country's new and growing textile industry. By then the Russians also were suspicious of Britain, which had a long-established base in India and was expanding its empire northward. The imperial competition between Russia and Britain would intensify in the

1870s and 1880s and cause several dangerous international crises. Russians also were concerned about their countrymen, mainly settlers on the steppe, who had been captured by Turkic tribes and sold into slavery. While this situation may have been little more than an excuse for expansion, it struck a raw nerve of national pride and inspired public anger. Russians, who were Orthodox Christians, were being enslaved by Muslims, who many Russians considered "heathens." Worse still, from the Russian Orthodox point of view, those captives sometimes converted to Islam. Finally, the Russians were driven by a sense of manifest destiny and a long-standing hostility to the Turkic peoples who lived to their south and east, with whom they had fought literally uncounted wars and battles over the centuries.

The conflict between religions, while secondary to the struggle for power and control, was felt by both sides. The Muslims of Central Asia looked down on the Christians intruding on their land from the west and at various times called for jihad, or holy war, against Russian "infidels." During the first decade of the 19th century, the ruler of Kokand warned against the danger they posed. He called on other Central Asian leaders "to conduct campaigns in defense or furtherance of Islam . . . as well as jihad against the worthless herd and gird our loins in hostility to them." More calls for holy war against Russia came in subsequent decades as Central Asian khanates found themselves under increasing pressure from the huge empire to the west.

The Russian Conquest of Southern Central Asia

Russian expansion in Central Asia slowed in the 1850s, as the empire's attention was focused on Europe. Between 1853 and 1856, the Russians were defeated in the Crimean War, which they fought against several European powers. This defeat stymied their efforts to expand their territory and influence on the west coast of the Black Sea and in the Balkan Peninsula. The Russians did better east of the Black Sea. By the end of the decade they had, against strong resistance, completed their conquest of the Caucasus region between the Black and Caspian Seas. Then the outbreak of the American Civil War cut off vital cotton supplies from the

United States. The stage had been set for a vigorous new campaign to complete the occupation of Central Asia.

There was not much standing in the way of a determined Russian drive. The three states that controlled most of southern Central Asia—the khanate of Kokand, the emirate of Bukhara, and the khanate of Khiva—were in poor shape. They were socially, politically, and economically backward societies. Most of the land was controlled by the state, by powerful landlords, or by Muslim religious institutions and was farmed by poor peasants. As tenants, they had to turn over between half and four-fifths of their crop to their landlords. The three states, under their absolute rulers, were constantly quarreling with each other and lacked well-defined borders. Bukhara and Kokand in particular were having difficulty controlling some of their outlying provinces. Ruled by Uzbek dynasties, all had relatively small and ethnically mixed populations. The emir of Bukhara ruled about 2.5 million people, about half Uzbeks, one-third Tajiks, and one-tenth Turkmen. Kokand had about 3 million people, mainly Uzbeks, Kazakhs, and Kyrgyz. Kokand, the best organized of these states, was also the smallest; its population of about 750,000 was made up mainly of Turkmen, Kazakhs, Uzbeks, and a group called Karakalpaks (a group related to the Kazakhs and Uzbeks and whose name means "Black Hat").

The bulk of that campaign was completed in about a decade. After taking Tashkent, the Russians conquered the city of Bukhara in 1867 and took Samarkand the next year. They then annexed some of Bukhara's territory and turned what was left into a protectorate, a status that left Russia with the control it wanted while the local ruler was allowed to manage local affairs. The khanate of Khiva met the same fate in 1873. In 1876, Russia abolished the khanate of Kokand, annexing all of its territory. Kokand's demise was not unwelcome to some Central Asians. It was, like the other states in the region, a tyranny, and during the 1850s and 1860s Kyrgyz tribes ruled by Kokand had appealed to Russian authorities for protection. In 1862, Kyrgyz soldiers fought with the Russians to take a fort that later became the city of Bishkek, the capital of present-day Kyrgyzstan.

Only the territory of present-day Turkmenistan remained beyond Russian control, and there the resistance turned out to be stubborn. The last bitter battle between the Russians and the Turkmen was fought in 1881 at a fortress called Goktere. Two years earlier, the Russians had been beaten badly in their attempt to take the place. On their second try, the

Russians mustered 11,000 men and 100 cannons for the siege. An estimated 14,500 Turkmen died. Many of them were civilians who the Russians massacred at the end of the battle. Three years later the Russians occupied Merv, completing their conquest of Central Asia. A series of Russian-British agreements followed to demarcate the borders between their two empires. The last, in 1897, attached a long skinny strip of land to Afghanistan between the Pamir and Hindu Kush mountains. This so-called Afghan finger, or Walkan Corridor, extended from northeastern Afghanistan to China, separating the two empires. It remains on maps today along the southern border of Tajikistan, an odd geographic leftover from Europe's age of imperialism.

Central Asia under Czarist Rule

In effect, Central Asia was a Russian colony. The Russians divided Central Asia into two main parts. The old name Turkestan was revived to designate the southern half of the region, now called the Governate-General of Turkestan. It included all of present-day Turkmenistan, Uzbekistan, Tajikistan, and Kyrgyzstan, parts of Kazakhstan. This large area was subdivided into several administrative units. The northern half, most of present-day Kazakhstan, was governed separately as the Steppe District and was likewise divided into several units. In both north and south, the Russians generally were content to control the region and exploit it for their economic needs while allowing the local people to go about their daily lives without interference whenever possible. Russian settlers who came into the region, whether as farmers or town dwellers, tended to live apart from the Central Asians. The settlers came in large numbers. By 1917, the year the Russian monarchy collapsed, about 2 million Russians and Ukrainians had moved into the region.

The main Russian economic goal was to increase cotton production. The Russians repaired old irrigation systems and built new ones to supply their expanded cotton fields. As a result, cotton production in the last two decades of the 19th century increased eightfold. Russians in Central Asia profited from growing cotton. Others in Moscow, St. Petersburg, and other cities in European Russia made money manufacturing cotton textiles. Central Asians, however, paid dearly for this development: They

The Russians marked their presence in Central Asia with Orthodox churches, such as this one on the Kazakh steppe in the early 20th century. (Courtesy Library of Congress)

lost the ability to grow food locally. Fields that had once produced grains, fruits, and vegetables were converted to cotton, especially in the fertile Fergana Valley, forcing Central Asians to import much of the food they ate. Nomads suffered in yet another way. As early as the mid-19th century, Russian forts on the steppe had begun blocking the nomads' ability to move their herds from pasture to pasture. As the century drew to a close, increasing sections of those pastures were converted to farms by Russian settlers. The new farmers displaced not only Kazakh nomads of the steppe, but also Kyrgyz nomads farther south in mountainous areas.

Two new railroads increased the pace of change and the number of settlers in the area. The first, the Trans-Caspian Railway, initially ran from Russia to Ashgabat. It was extended to Samarkand in 1888, and from there to Tashkent. The second railroad entered Central Asia from the north, finally reaching Tashkent in 1905. Aided by the new railroads, Russian and Ukrainian settlers established half a million farms in northern and eastern Kazakhstan between 1906 and 1912. Kazakhstan was being used by Russian authorities to solve the land shortage problem among Russian peasants.

There were a few positive aspects to Russian rule in Central Asia. The region enjoyed greater peace and security, as the old native conflicts were kept under control. Along with railroads, a few industrial enterprises were built, generally plants to process food or produce textiles from cotton. However, workers in these factories frequently were Russian immigrants to the region. Some secular schools were established, their main purpose being to train a local elite that knew Russian, shared Russian values, and would help the Russian authorities govern the region. While little was done to combat illiteracy, the arrival of the Russians led to the first publication of books in the Kyrgyz language.

Opposition to Russian Rule

There were a number of revolts against Russian rule in various parts of Central Asia between the mid-1880s and the turn of the century. All were put down quickly and brutally. Investigations into these revolts led the Russian authorities to pay closer attention to potentially dangerous ways of thinking, especially those with appeal across ethnic lines. They came in two varieties: traditional Islamic teachings and a more modern outlook based on pan-Turkic ideas. The Russians at first were more concerned with the teachings of pan-Islamic clerics, but by the turn of the century a pan-Turkic movement had emerged as the greater threat. It was known as Jadidism, the name taken from the Arabic phrase *usul-i-jadid,* meaning "new method," a phrase that applied specifically to a new method of education. The Jadids were young men from wealthy Central Asian families who often had been educated in Russian universities or in Turkey, where they had been exposed to modern ideas. They believed that Central Asia could only achieve its independence and protect its culture if it gained advanced knowledge and modernized. That in turn meant modernizing not only Central Asian society, but Islam as well, an attitude that did not sit well with Muslim religious authorities.

The Jadids were excited by the Revolution of 1905 in Russia, which raised the prospect of democratic reforms and even the possibility that Russian rule might be overthrown. The defeat of the revolutionary forces dashed those hopes in Central Asia, even though there were important, if limited, political reforms in Russia. The Jadids had to content themselves with founding new schools to spread their message. They started more than a 100 of these schools in the decade after 1905. Interestingly, while Russian authorities certainly tried to limit its influence, the greatest opposition to the Jadid movement came from the local religious and conservative secular elites who feared the new ideas threatened their positions of leadership.

Although the Jadids were kept in check, there was widespread discontent in Central Asia by the first decade of the 20th century. Farmers who had been driven from their land, nomads who saw their way of life threatened by spreading cotton farms, and a small but growing local intelligentsia with modern ideas all resented Russian rule. There was ample reason for complaint. By the time the Russian Revolution broke out in 1917, Russian and Ukrainian settlers had seized an estimated 100 million acres of Kazakh land. There were famines among the Muslim people of Central Asia every year from 1910 to 1913. None of them even had status as citizens of the empire that had taken their land. The Russian word to describe their official status, *inorodsty*, means "foreign subjects" or "alien-born."

This Turkmen posing proudly with his camel early in the 20th century probably was transporting grain or cotton. (Courtesy Library of Congress)

The outbreak of World War I in 1914 brought more hardships to every part of the Russian Empire, including Central Asia. Once the war began, new taxes that fell heavily on an overwhelmingly poor population intensified discontent. The only saving grace was that the region's Muslim men were not conscripted to fight in the war. That changed in mid-1916 when the government issued a decree calling for Central Asian men between the ages of 18 and 43 to be drafted to work in labor battalions. The decree was a disaster. Central Asians were conscripted into a war in which they clearly had no stake. Further, Russians told these men, who took pride in their martial traditions and skills, that they were not fit to fight but suited only for digging trenches or performing similar nonmilitary tasks.

The decree sparked an uprising in Kazakhstan that quickly spread across Central Asia. This reaction was not a surprise to local Russian authorities. For the past three years they had been warning that the government's treatment of the Kazakhs was creating an explosive situation. Within a few months, about 50,000 rebels had taken up arms. Russian troops were called in to suppress the rebellion, which they did by the end of the year with great brutality and at the cost of many lives. Entire settlements were burned to the ground. Russian settlers in the region, who had suffered at least 2,000 dead at rebel hands, took advantage of the revolt to seize more land. About 300,000 Kazakh and Kyrgyz nomads were driven from the lands on which they had pastured their herds. Approximately 250,000 people from both groups fled to China and Mongolia or starved to death. It has been estimated that more than 100,000 people were killed in Kyrgyzstan alone, making this one of the worst periods in Kyrgyz history.

The suppression of the rebellion of 1916 turned out to be the last act of oppression Central Asians would suffer at the hands of the Russian Empire. In March of 1917, the hardship caused by World War I sparked another upheaval, this one in St. Petersburg (called Petrograd at the time), the Russian capital. The czarist government collapsed, and a new government, committed to democracy, came to power. For a short time it looked as if a new and better time had come to Russia, and to Central Asia. But Russia's new democratic government was overthrown within eight months by a group of radical socialist revolutionaries who had no use for democracy. They accepted no opposition, either. This seizure of power by a militant minority determined to totally remake Russia ushered in an era of repression and hardship that far exceeded anything known under the czars.

NOTES

p. 35 "The Russians come from the North, Kokand . . ." Quoted in Martha Brill Olcott, *The Kazakhs* (Stanford, Calif.: Hoover Institution Press, 1987), p. 65.

p. 36 " 'to conduct campaigns in defense of . . .' " Quoted in Edward Allworth, "Encounter," in Edward Allworth, editor, *Central Asia: 130 Years of Russian Dominance, A Historical Overview* (Durham and London: Duke University Press, 1994), p. 7.

4

SOVIET CENTRAL ASIA, 1917 TO 1985

The Revolution of March 1917 overthrew the government of the czar and put an end to the Russian Empire. The old regime was replaced by what the Russians called the Provisional Government, whose leaders expected to govern Russia until a permanent government, based on a new constitution, could be put in place. The new government's leaders were reformers and moderates. They intended for Russia to become a parliamentary democracy with a free-enterprise economic system; in other words, they hoped to see Russia follow the example of the countries of Western Europe. At the same time, they were Russian nationalists, which meant that in their view a new democratic Russia would keep approximately the same borders as the old Russian Empire. Precisely how they would do this and remain consistent with the democratic principle of national self-determination was unclear. Nor was it clear which of the many non-Russians within borders established by generations of expansion and conquest—about half of the total population—would want to be a part of the new democratic Russian state.

Most Russians, at least among the educated and urban classes, greeted the March revolution with relief. Despite fears of instability, there was reasonably widespread consensus that the country was better off having rid itself of the czar and czarism. Russia, to be sure, was still suffering from its losses during World War I, but there was optimism that it finally had leaders at the helm who were competent, understood the problems the country faced, and were concerned about the welfare of the population.

That optimism did not last. The Provisional Government, its good intentions notwithstanding, suffered more defeats on the battlefield and failed to restore order in Russia's cities and villages. Casualties and economic hardship caused by the war continued to mount. On November 7, 1917, the struggle for control of Russia entered a new stage. In one of the most important events of the 20th century, a small group of radical socialists called the Bolsheviks took advantage of the chaos and overthrew the Provisional Government in an armed coup. The Bolsheviks followed the ideas of a 19th-century German socialist thinker named Karl Marx. They rejected democracy. They wanted to rule alone and began suppressing other political groups as soon as they had seized power. Even more important, their goal was to overhaul Russia completely and turn it into the world's first socialist society. Private property would be abolished and the entire economy would be controlled by the state. The Bolsheviks had no use for democracy because they assumed that they represented the will of the Russian working class, the only class that mattered. They further assumed that they represented all progressive forces in history. They considered free elections a threat since the people as a whole could easily be misled. The party's leader, Vladimir I. Lenin, was shrewd, flexible, tough, and ruthless in a time of crisis and rapid change. Nor was Russia, which covered one-sixth of the world's land surface, big enough for Bolshevik dreams. The Bolshevik Party leaders saw their revolution in Russia as only the first event in a chain reaction that eventually would engulf the entire world.

The Bolshevik coup quickly plunged Russia into a dreadful civil war that lasted until the end of 1920. Most of the active political groups in Russia—from moderate socialists to liberals to conservative monarchists—opposed the Bolsheviks. They did not want to see their country subject to a radical one-party dictatorship. During the civil war these groups collectively were called the Whites—the Bolsheviks were known as the Reds and called their military force the Red Army—but the Whites never were able to unite effectively. This failure helped the Bolsheviks win the civil war and hold on to power. The civil war was far more destructive than even World War I and left the country in ruins. During the turmoil a few national groups in the western part of the old empire—the Poles, Finns, Latvians, Lithuanians, and Estonians—

managed to break away and establish their independence. The rest of the former empire, including Central Asia, remained in Bolshevik hands. The Bolshevik experiment of building socialism under a one-party dictatorship soon evolved into a totalitarian state. It caused levels of hardship and oppression worse than anything that had occurred under the czars.

The Russian Revolution in Central Asia

Central Asia's Muslims were not involved in either of Russia's two 1917 revolutions. The long-standing local tensions between Russians and Muslims were overshadowed at first by the immediate struggle for power between rival groups of Russians. The key arena in Central Asia was Tashkent, the region's largest city and former administrative center for southern Central Asia, the area the czarist regime had called Turkestan. When the Provisional Government was set up in March 1917 in Petrograd, supporters of the new regime set up a committee in Tashkent to act as a local government and carry out its policies. Mirroring what had occurred in St. Petersburg, a number of socialist groups set up what they called a council—the Russian word was *soviet*—to represent the interests of the region's workers and socialists. In practice, the soviet was both a rival to the Tashkent committee and a limit to what it could do. Significantly, most of the people on these bodies and the people they said they represented were Russians.

Muslims were largely ignored by the squabbling Russians. Yet the March Revolution that had swept away czarism and its political police had created conditions in which Muslims with nationalist views could express them more openly. Well aware they would have to act on their own if they wanted to influence events, Central Asian Muslims with a variety of nationalist views began calling meetings and setting up their own organizations. During the spring of 1917, some of them produced a mildly nationalist program calling for an autonomous, though not independent, Turkestan within a democratic Russia. Their program also called for putting the new Turkestan under Muslim religious law, without explaining how that could be reconciled with democracy. Muslim nationalists also called for replacing the cultivation of cotton, to them a symbol of Russian colonialism, with grains and other crops.

On November 7, 1917, the political landscape suddenly shifted when the Bolsheviks overthrew the Provisional Government in Petrograd. Bolsheviks in Tashkent, who several days earlier had taken control of the city, responded by announcing the establishment of the Turkestan Council of People's Commissars (the official name of the Bolshevik government in Petrograd was the Council of People's Commissars). But Muslim leaders by then had their own plans for Central Asia. In December, they announced the formation of their own government in the city of Kokand, the Muslim Provisional Government of Autonomous Turkestan. The Muslims immediately came into conflict with the Bolshevik government in Tashkent and its bosses in Petrograd. In theory, there should not have been a conflict. As revolutionaries supposedly committed to freedom for all oppressed peoples, the Bolsheviks after seizing power in November had issued a proclamation promising the Muslim people of Russia that "From now on your beliefs and customs, your national and cultural institutions are being declared free and inviolable." In reality, the new Bolshevik* government was as determined to keep control of Central Asia as the czarist regime or Provisional Government had. It demonstrated its real intentions when its soldiers overthrew the Muslim Kokand government in February 1918, killing many innocent people in the process. A Kazakh government in the northern steppe, set up in December 1917, met the same fate, albeit somewhat later. Lacking financial resources or an army, it survived as a phantom government until the Bolsheviks liquidated it in 1920.

The delay in dealing with the Kazakh government occurred because the Bolsheviks were fighting for their own survival in the civil war between 1918 and 1920. In their desperate effort to win that war, they resorted to drastic measures that made them enemies throughout Russia, including among the Muslims of Central Asia. One of the most notorious Bolshevik tactics was seizing food from farmers to feed their army, a policy they followed in all the territory they controlled. In Central Asia that policy, combined with the harsh winter of 1918–19, helped cause a famine in which at least 1 million people starved to death, the great

---

*When referring to the period 1917 to 1924, it is common to use the terms *Bolshevik*, *Soviet*, and *Communist* interchangeably for the regime established on November 7, 1917. This volume will use the terms *Bolshevik* or *Soviet* for the period November 1917 to 1924, and the terms *Soviet* and *Communist* for the period 1924 to December 1991.

majority of whom were Muslims. The Bolsheviks also forced peasants in Central Asia to give up their cotton crop, shooting those who refused to cooperate. These and other measures provoked a revolt that spread to all of southern Central Asia. In some places the upheaval lasted much longer than the civil war itself.

THE BASMACHI REVOLT

The Central Asian rebellion against the Bolshevik regime is known as the Basmachi Revolt. It was led by traditional conservative Muslim religious figures called mullahs and clan notables. The rebellion was provoked by Bolshevik repression and secular reforms that threatened to undermine the region's traditional way of life. The Muslims' goal was to protect their way of life by expelling Russians, and other Europeans, from Central Asia. After that, their objectives differed. Some groups fought to establish strict Islamic rule, others in the name of Turkic nationalism, still others mostly against communism. Russians named the movement *basmachi,* a pejorative term meaning "bandit." Although it could justifiably be applied to many of the independent armed groups that participated in the movement, the term was not a fair description of all of them.

The revolt began in the Fergana Valley and eventually drew support from many Uzbek, Turkmen, Tajiks, and Kyrgyz groups. The Basmachi fought a disorganized, guerrilla war. Bands fighting under its banner operated independently and rarely coordinated their actions. Local rivalries and changing conditions often caused shifting alliances that hampered resistance against the Bolsheviks. Still, the Basmachi fought effectively enough. They were very difficult to defeat. At one point during 1919, they controlled the entire Fergana Valley. The Bolsheviks eventually had to send more than 100,000 soldiers to defeat them. That force arrived in the region in 1920, after the civil war against the Whites was largely won. It was led by Mikhail Frunze, one of the most skilled and successful Red Army commanders, who happened to have been born in Bishkek. Also on the scene was the Red Army's commander-in-chief and its most famous calvary officer, Semyon Budennyi. The Bolsheviks used nonmilitary measures that undermined support for the Basmachi. They stopped seizing food from farmers, lowered taxes, and ended anti-Islamic policies.

They promised land reform and skillfully exploited rivalries between the Basmachi commanders.

During 1922 and 1923, most Basmachi resistance was broken. In the summer of 1922 the Bolsheviks succeeded in killing the most famous rebel commander, a former general and political leader from Turkey named Enver Pasha. His death marked the end of a bizarre career. As a soldier of the Ottoman Empire, Pasha had been the general in charge of the genocidal massacre of more than 1 million Armenians during World War I. He then came to Russia and cast his lot with the Bolsheviks, accepting their assignment to go to Central Asia to deal with the Basmachis. Soon after arriving he decided to switch sides. Enver Pasha finally was killed in a minor battle by the regime he had just betrayed.

In the wake of their defeat, thousands of Basmachi fighters and their families fled to Afghanistan. Yet some guerrilla resistance continued until the end of the decade in Tajikistan, and the memory of the Basmachi resistance lingered among Central Asians well beyond that. Still, after bitter fighting, by the early 1920s the Bolshevik regime was in a position to reorganize Central Asia as it saw fit.

The Soviet Republics of Central Asia

One of the many urgent problems the Bolshevik government faced after the civil war was how to govern a country that remained a multinational empire. To be successful, they had to reconcile competing needs. They wanted to maintain tight central control over the entire country, but they also wanted to give the impression that its many non-Russian subjects were equal members of a new socialist and fraternal union. Their solution was a new political phenomenon: the Union of Soviet Socialist Republics (USSR or Soviet Union), which officially came into existence in December 1922. The new union officially had a federal structure, something like the United States, composed of member "union" republics. The Russian republic—officially the Russian Soviet Federated Socialist Republic (RSFSR)—was the largest. It was subdivided into smaller regions for ethnic minorities living within its borders, some called "autonomous republics" and others, with less status, called "autonomous regions." There were also union republics for Ukrainians (the Ukrainian Soviet

Socialist Republic), for Belarusans (or Belorussians), and for the people of the Caucasus region (the Transcaucasian Republic). This setup was primarily for the sake of appearance. In reality, the Soviet Union was a dictatorship tightly controlled from the center by the Communist Party (as the Bolshevik Party had been renamed in 1918). The federal structure of the Soviet Union was an administrative ploy to hide the dictatorship's true nature. Yet restructuring provided a way to govern the Soviet Union, especially as efforts were made to enlist non-Russians into the Communist Party and thereby into the tightly knit apparatus that controlled the huge country.

Having established the framework it needed, the Soviet government turned to Central Asia. It began by using ethnicity and borders to undermine any competing authority in the region. The Soviets were worried that Central Asia's Muslim community would be attracted to outside Islamic influences. It especially feared pan-Islamism, the idea that all Islamic peoples were a single community and should live that way. The Soviets, who considered religion a superstition that stood in the way of progress, also wanted to combat the conservative Muslim forces in Central Asia which opposed socialism and other secular reforms, such as equal rights for women. So they did two things: first, they divided the region up into five ethnic units, one each for the Kazakhs, Uzbeks, Turkmen, Tajiks, and Kyrgyz; second, they drew borders that left pockets of one ethnic group within the borders of another's unit, thereby creating friction points that prevented any united front from developing against the ruling Communist Party based in Moscow (the country's capital since 1918).

The system put in place in 1924 created five new units: two new union republics and three autonomous republics. The Uzbek Soviet Socialist Republic and the Turkmen Soviet Socialist Republic were the two union republics. The Kazakhs, Kyrgyz, and Tajiks all received autonomous republics, the first two as part of the RSFSR and the third as part of the Uzbek SSR. In 1929, the Tajik autonomous republic was separated from the Uzbek SSR and elevated to a union republic, a status achieved by the Kazakh and Kyrgyz republics in 1936. The borders of the Central Asian union republics helped make all local ethnic groups dependent on Moscow. Samarkand and Bukhara, both traditional Tajik cultural centers, ended up in Uzbekistan. The Fergana Valley was split between the Uzbek, Tajik, and Kyrgyz republics. The Uzbek republic got most of it but in a way that divided ethnic groups, clans, and villages, with the largely Uzbek city of Osh at the eastern end of the valley ending up in the Kyrgyz republic. Further north, the borders of the Kazakh republic were drawn to include the large Slavic populations in the northern and eastern steppes.

At the same time, other devices, dating from the 1920s and modified and perfected over time, were used to bind the Muslims of Central Asia to the Soviet state. One method was administrative. Unlike in most countries, where the government exercises power, real power in the Soviet Union lay with the Communist Party.** Officially, the two were separate, but party leaders occupied every important government post. The party's structure paralleled the government's, from the national all the way down to the lowest local level. For each union republic (or autonomous republic) government, there was a parallel party organization. Communist Party members were carefully selected and vetted for loyalty to the Soviet system and always subject to the constant spying of the Soviet secret police. The Soviet regime made a major effort to recruit a native elite that would serve its interests in return for privilege and status. This was largely successful. Yet nothing was left to chance. Slavic officials often occupied key positions in union republic Communist parties. By the mid-1960s, a tradition emerged in which the top position, or first secretary, in union republic party organizations usually was given to a native. The number-two position usually went to a Russian or Ukrainian, whose most important function was to keep a close eye on the official who in theory was his boss.

The Soviets also regulated Muslims' use of their languages. Prior to the 20th century, the various Turkic dialects spoken across Central Asia tended to blend into one another. The Tajiks spoke a Persian dialect but used classical Persian as their literary language. Beginning in the 1920s, the Soviet government's language policies were designed to cut off the Central Asians from outside influences and simultaneously divide them from one another. One technique was to change the system used in writing these languages. The Arabic alphabet was replaced by the Latin alphabet, the same alphabet used to write languages such as English, French, and German. In fact, the Latin alphabet was better suited to both the Turkic and Iranian languages of Central Asia. But the main objective was to

---

**Its official name from 1952 was the Communist Party of the Soviet Union (CPSU). For most of the Soviet era the party leader was called the general secretary.

cut the Central Asians from their Islamic and Turkic or Iranian traditions. In 1940, the alphabet was changed again, this time to the Cyrillic alphabet used to write Russian and other Slavic languages. The aim was to strengthen Central Asia's ties with the Russian core of the Soviet Union.

Russian became the official language of each Central Asian republic. The goal was to make Central Asia's Muslim population more Russian, a policy called Russification. As in all non-Russian republics, Central Asian students had to study Russian. Many local places had their names changed to Russian ones. Aside from intentional government policies, Russification was promoted as loanwords from Russian gradually found their way into local languages.

The Stalin Era

The most important, and by far the most wrenching changes that came to Central Asia during the Soviet era did not have to do with tightening the region's political bonds to Moscow or with Russification. They resulted from the attempt to transform the Soviet Union's economy. Using Marxist principles, the Soviets instigated a program of rapid industrialization along centrally planned socialist lines. These policies had catastrophic consequences for all of the people of the Soviet Union, Russian and non-Russian alike. Scars from this time remain visible and painful to this day. This program was implemented under Joseph Stalin, the man who became the Soviet leader, and then the all-powerful dictator, after Lenin died. Lenin's death had been the signal for his lieutenants to change the name of St. Petersburg (called Petrograd from 1914 to 1924) to Leningrad (*grad* means city in Russian) in the dead leader's honor and then immediately begin a struggle for power to succeed him. Stalin had won that contest by 1929. His triumph led to an industrialization drive at breakneck speed. It was an enormous undertaking. The Soviet Union had inherited a semi-industrial economy that was backward by Western European standards. Stalin and the Communist Party leadership were determined to catch up with the West by making as much economic progress in the next decade as the West had made in the past century. They also were determined to use that new economic power to turn the Soviet Union into the world's leading military power. Stalin's plans called for phenomenal, and ultimately unrealistic, increases in industrial production. The greatest increases were planned for so-called heavy industries—such as steel, machine tools, and coal—upon which a modern industrial society, and a modern military, were based.

COLLECTIVIZATION AND FAMINE

Industrialization depended on overhauling agriculture, still the largest sector of the Soviet economy in the late 1920s. The problem was that most of the Soviet Union's food was grown on 20 million small and inefficient peasant farms. The goal, again following Marxist principles, was to combine these 20 million small farms into about 200,000 collective farms, which were large farms controlled by the Communist Party on which dozens or hundreds of families worked together. Soviet planners expected that these farms, with their large fields and herds of livestock, would make use of modern machinery and methods to produce much more food than under the old system. At the same time, the state would have control of what was produced and would use it to promote industrialization. Food would be supplied to workers building and working in new factories and exported to pay for modern machinery those factories needed.

Collectivization immediately ran into trouble when most peasants refused to give up their land. The Soviet regime responded with brutal and overwhelming force. Peasants were driven into the collectives, sometimes after bloody battles against soldiers armed with machine guns. The wealthier peasants, known as *kulaks*, met an even worse fate. Stalin had decided that by definition they were enemies of socialism. Kulak families therefore were driven from the countryside altogether. Millions of men, women, and children were shipped to forced labor camps or deported to remote areas of the country, where they were left penniless to fend for themselves. As a result of the violence and chaos, all made worse by the excessive speed at which collectivization was carried out, agricultural production during the 1930s dropped rather than increased.

One immediate consequence of collectivization in Ukraine and other European parts of the Soviet Union was the notorious "terror famine" of 1932–33. The famine was the result of a poor harvest and the government's insistence on taking almost all the peasants' grain to feed city workers or to be sent abroad to pay for new machines. Left without food, thousands of peasants began to starve. The government made no effort to stop what was happening. Rather, it denied that anyone in the Soviet Union was starving. The Stalin regime actually used the famine to break resistance to collectivization in the Ukraine. At least 5 million peasants, and possibly more, died during the famine.

Collectivization had equally disastrous consequences in Central Asia. The impact was worst on the Kazakh nomads, who suffered a twofold disaster. First, they were forced to give up their traditional way of life as wandering herders. Second, they were forced to join collective farms. As had occurred in the Russian and Ukrainian parts of the Soviet Union, nomads and peasants in Central Asia often killed their animals rather than give them up to the government. Others fought and killed the Communist Party workers who were seizing their property and destroying their lives. Millions of animals were either killed or died in the chaos of collectivization. Life was disrupted to the core. In some places, half the animals died within a matter of weeks. In just four years during the late 1920s and early 1930s, about 80 percent of the livestock animals in Kazakhstan were killed or died. The figure was almost as bad for Central Asia as a whole. An American on the scene described what he witnessed:

> When the Communist shock troops began to break up those herds and put pressure on the nomad owners to pool their animals in so-called collective farms, the latter simply killed their animals. The ex-nomads who survived this period were rounded up as the *kulaks* have been. . . . Many of them resisted dispossession; these were adjudged criminals, and sent to jail or shot.

Famine and flight followed. As of 1932, about a fifth of the population, many of whom had fled the collective farms, were homeless, wandering on the steppe without their animals or any means of providing for themselves. The best guess is that 1.5 million Kazakhs starved during the 1930s, and there was serious famine among the Kyrgyz as well. Hundreds of thousands of nomads fled the steppe and Kazakhstan altogether, most of them going to Uzbekistan and Turkmenistan. There they joined with local people in a new upsurge of the Basmachi revolt.

Despite the chaos and resistance, the Soviet government succeeded in collectivizing agriculture in Central Asia by 1932. It had won its war with the people of the region. By the end of the decade, hundreds of thousands of Kazakhs who had once been nomads had been settled on collective farms. Only a small number continued to live as nomads. However, as elsewhere, production from the collective farms was disappointingly low. It would take more than 30 years—until the 1960s—for the livestock herds to be restored to their pre-collectivization numbers.

THE GREAT PURGE

The other enormous Soviet storm that swept Central Asia during the 1930s is known as the Great Purge. It was a tidal wave of arrests and murders that began in late 1934 and reached a peak between 1936 and 1938. The Great Purge was Stalin's attempt to destroy any possible opposition to his dictatorship, first within the Communist Party and then among the Soviet people as a whole. Millions of people were arrested on trumped up charges. They were forced to confess after long periods of physical and psychological abuse and torture. Most ended up in the Soviet Union's vast network of labor camps, where they died in enormous numbers. More than a million were shot. In Central Asia, as elsewhere in the Soviet Union, the purge swept through the ranks of the party, the educated elite, and the population as a whole. Among the purge's high-ranking victims was Faizullah Khojaev, the Communist leader of Uzbekistan from 1924 to 1937. He was tried in 1938 in Moscow with other top party leaders in one of three major public show trials Stalin staged between 1936 and 1938. Found guilty of the absurd charge that he had worked to overthrow the Soviet regime, Khojaev was executed immediately after the trial ended. Another victim of the Great Purge was Törekul Aitmatov, father of Chingiz Aitmatov, the Kyrgyz novelist who has achieved the most international recognition of any contemporary Central Asian writer. The elder Aitmatov, a loyal Communist Party member, was arrested and sent to a labor camp, where he died like millions of other innocent victims of Stalin's Great Purge.

WORLD WAR II

The one Soviet disaster that did not hit Central Asia with its full force was World War II. Central Asians, to be sure, were drafted to fight in the

These members of a youth brigade worked in the Karaganda coal field in the late 1940s. The raw materials of Kazakhstan were very important to the Soviet economy. (Courtesy Library of Congress)

war, and like other Soviet soldiers suffered high casualty rates. But geography at least had some mercy on Central Asia during the war. World War II began for the Soviet Union when Nazi Germany invaded the country in June 1941. The Germans swept eastward to the gates of Moscow, Leningrad, and Stalingrad (a city on the Volga River that Stalin had renamed after himself). The areas they overran were devastated, and millions of civilians were killed. But met by heroic and often unbelievable resistance, the Germans never took those three key cities. Beginning with the Soviet victory at Stalingrad in early 1943, they were turned back and driven from the Soviet Union before they could reach Central Asia.

Meanwhile, industrialization of the region, which began during the 1930s, received an enormous boost during the war. Hundreds of factories in the path of the invaders were meticulously disassembled and moved piece by piece from European parts of the country to Central Asia. There they were reassembled and immediately enlisted in the desperate war effort. The war also brought temporary relief from certain repressive policies. During the 1920s and 1930s, the Soviet regime had waged a campaign against Islam in Central Asia as part of its overall attack on religion throughout the country. That changed during the war, when the regime was desperate to win popular support. In Russian parts of the country, the regime made a peace of sorts with the Russian Orthodox Church. In Central Asia the effort to suppress Islam, which had included closing schools, mosques, and Islamic courts, was scaled back. Some schools and mosques were allowed to reopen, and a Muslim Board of Central Asia was established in Tashkent as part of the effort to improve the government's relationship with Muslim religious leaders. These concessions, like others Stalin permitted during the war, were rescinded after the war ended in 1945.

Khrushchev and the Virgin Lands, 1953–1964

Stalin died in 1953. His death, like Lenin's, was followed by a struggle for power among his top lieutenants. At the same time, there was a period of political reform. Stalin's successors generally agreed that certain intolerable aspects of life under the dictator had to end. Nobody had been safe. Even after the end of the Great Purge in 1938, anyone—from the highest official to the ordinary worker and peasant—was subject to arrest without cause. These arrests were carried out by the secret police, which operated directly under Stalin's control. Within months of Stalin's death his secret police chief had been arrested and by the end of the year executed. Reforms were put in place in 1953 to make sure that no leader, even the man who emerged at the top as the Communist Party leader and as the most powerful political figure in the Soviet Union, would have anything near Stalin's power. The dictatorship of one man was turned into a dictatorship of the party leadership, similar to what had existed before Stalin's rise to power.

The man who won the struggle for power after Stalin's death was Nikita Khrushchev, a tough peasant-born party boss who had served as head of both the Moscow and Ukrainian party organizations. Khrushchev had become convinced that the Soviet Union had to make major reforms that went far beyond what was done immediately after Stalin's death.

They included economic reforms designed to raise the miserably low standard of living. Under Stalin, all resources had been poured into heavy industry and into the military. Soviet people needed more food, especially grain. Realizing that goal would have a huge impact on Central Asia, in particular Kazakhstan.

Khrushchev's program to increase grain production was called the Virgin Lands campaign. It called for plowing up millions of acres of land on the steppes of Kazakhstan and western Siberia. These areas had not been planted before for good reason: Despite their fertile soil, the rainfall in the area was too light and irregular to sustain agriculture on a long-term basis, averaging only between 8 and 16 inches (200 to 400 millimeters) per year. If the rains failed, and the region's climatic history guaranteed that sooner or later they would, then the region would be turned into a huge dust bowl.

The Virgin Lands program was launched in 1954, over the objection of local Kazakh party leaders, who were replaced because of their opposition. Three hundred thousand Russian and Ukrainian volunteers were recruited and sent to the Virgin Lands. There they were settled on what were called state farms, which were similar to collective farms but with two differences: They were much larger and their workers were paid in wages rather than according to a formula based on how much the farm produced. In a project that resembled a military campaign, 50,000 tractors, 6,000 trucks, and other agricultural equipment were shipped to Central Asia. In the next few years, almost 50 million acres of Kazakh steppe was plowed up and planted with grain, as were millions of additional acres in western Siberia. After a disappointing year in 1955, the next year yielded a bumper harvest. The years that followed saw mixed results: a bad year in 1957, when it was dry; and an excellent year in 1958, when the rains were more plentiful. By the early 1960s the rainfall realities of the region began to take their toll. In 1963, dry conditions and winds of up to 95 miles (152 km) per hour turned the Kazakh steppe into a dust bowl. Topsoil was blown away and millions of acres of farmland ruined. Entire towns were covered with silt. It was a major ecological disaster. That did not stop the Virgin Lands enterprise. Until the collapse of the Soviet Union in 1991, Kazakhstan produced one-third of the country's wheat.

The Virgin Lands program upset many Kazakhs in another way as well. It brought more than 1.5 million Russians and Ukrainians into

Kazakhstan and several other parts of Central Asia. At the time Kazakhs were a minority in their own union republic. The influx of more outsiders threatened to make that status permanent. It turned out that this concern was premature. The migration associated with the Virgin Lands project was the last major influx of Russians and other Europeans into the region, and it was not long before the high Kazakh birthrate began to shift the population balance in their favor.

Farther south, the impact of another Soviet agricultural project was less easily reversed. Ever since the 19th century, Russia had been promoting cotton cultivation in Central Asia, despite the demands that this thirsty crop put on the water resources of the region. That effort continued and expanded under the Soviet regime. Production rose dramatically during the 1920s and 1930s, and by 1931 the Soviet Union was self-sufficient in cotton. By 1937 it was an exporter. In 1938 cotton production in Uzbekistan was more than double what it had been in 1913, the year before the start of World War I. Until the 1960s, however, the irrigation needs of the cotton fields did not noticeably affect the Aral Sea, even with about 50,000 square kilometers under irrigation. The impact on the sea increased substantially when the Garagum and other new canals began drawing water from the Amu Darya and Syr Darya rivers after 1959. By the late 1970s, Central Asia was growing 95 percent of the Soviet Union's cotton. In Uzbekistan, the cotton industry—growing and processing the so-called "white gold"—accounted for almost two-thirds of the economy and employed about 40 percent of the republic's labor force. But the price was dreadfully high. The substantial loss of water took its toll. Because of poor construction and other inefficiencies, half the water that entered the Garagum Canal leaked out before reaching cotton fields. The Aral Sea was denied most of the water it had been receiving in the 1950s and began to dry up, with disastrous ecological consequences that have not been reversed.

The Brezhnev Era and Corruption, 1964–1985

In 1964, Nikita Khrushchev was removed from office. Khrushchev fell because many of his economic policies had failed and because some of his reforms threatened the privileges and positions of many top Communist Party officials. Party leaders who had once supported him turned against him, and in October 1964 the party's top decision-making body voted to replace him with Leonid Brezhnev. Brezhnev was a Khrushchev protégé who had turned against his mentor. He had served as the party leader in Kazakhstan from 1954 to 1956, the crucial early days of the Virgin Lands campaign. By 1964, Brezhnev and the rest of the Communist Party elite wanted security and stability above all else. This required raising the country's standard of living and easing tensions with the United States, both of which the Brezhnev regime made serious efforts to do. It also meant there could be no reforms that might threaten the good life enjoyed by the party elite. In effect, it meant that many problems plaguing the Soviet Union were left unchecked. Among the most serious were an economy that was over-centralized and increasingly inefficient, and widespread corruption. Brezhnev and his colleagues did nothing about either of these problems. They grew worse each year. By the 1980s, they had reached crisis proportions.

One dangerous consequence of these developments was growing economic inequality. The Soviet Union was supposed to be a socialist society whose most important principle was that society's wealth was distributed equally. That had never been true, but under Brezhnev it became increasingly difficult to hide the truth. This was especially obvious in Central Asia, where the standard of living for ordinary people was the lowest in the Soviet Union but where party leaders lived almost like the khans of old. Corruption in Central Asia ran deep. Modern Soviet-style corruption was layered over centuries of old-fashioned clan politics in which traditional leaders demanded and received tribute for the favors they dispensed. None of this bothered the authorities in Moscow, who were content to let local Central Asian leaders make their personal profits so long as they maintained order and delivered the goods the central government needed.

This model of dual corruption applied well to Dinmukhamed Kunayev, the party chief in Kazakhstan from 1964 until 1986. In 1971, he became the first Kazakh to reach the Politburo, the Communist Party's most powerful body. His tenure had its positive aspects. Educational reforms increased the number of native Kazakhs attending universities. The capital city of Almaty grew into a relatively prosperous large city. But

Dinmukhamed Kunayev ran Kazakhstan for the Soviet leadership for more than 20 years, often sacrificing local interests to those of the Communist Party bosses in Moscow. (AP/Wide World Photos)

Kunayev made no effort to oppose Soviet policies such as its atomic tests that were damaging the environment and the health of the people. He delivered what Moscow wanted and in return was allowed to run Kazakhstan in a way that enriched himself and those around him. Nothing was too good for them, especially those closest to the party leader. Once when his wife became jealous over an expensive Japanese tea set that the wife of another party leader had received, Kunayev arranged for his private plane—at his disposal for his tasks as a member of the Politburo—to fly to the Soviet far east. It brought back, as a Western journalist reported, "not only dozens of Japanese tea sets but also Japanese sound and video equipment, furs, carvings on rare deer horn—the finest art of indigenous craftsmen—thousands of jars of Pacific crab and other fruits of the ocean." Kunayev finally was forced to retire "for reasons of health" when the reformer Mikhail Gorbachev came to power, but even then he continued to live in luxury, across the street from a park named in his honor.

For all his extravagance, Kunayev was no match for his Uzbek neighbor and colleague Sharaf Rashidov, a master of nepotism and corruption. Rashidov, Uzbekistan's party boss from 1959 to 1983, headed a mafia-style network that looted billions of dollars from the local economy. Rashidov and other high-ranking party officials took regular pay-offs to ignore illegal activities. They sold prestigious and powerful jobs. They also arranged, for a price, for not-guilty verdicts in trials. The rates for not-guilty verdicts were well known: The chairman of the parliament demanded 100,000 rubles for a pardon for a serious felony, the president of the supreme court charged 25,000 to 100,000 rubles.

Rashidov's grandest scheme, carried out with full knowledge of party leaders in Moscow, was to overstate the local cotton crop and get paid by Moscow for cotton that was never grown. An estimated $2 billion flowed from Moscow into the private coffers of Rashidov and his cronies. In return, Rashidov sent planeloads of expensive gifts to the appropriate bosses in Moscow. When he died in 1983, Rashidov was buried with honors.

One of Rashidov's closest associates was Akhmadzhan Adylov, head of the party organization in the Feranga Valley for two decades. Adylov was known as the Godfather and claimed to be a descendant of Tamerlane, a claim that his infamous cruelty almost made believable. In a region where most people lived in poverty, a Western journalist reported, Adylov lived "on a vast estate with peacocks, lions, thoroughbred horses, concubines, and a slave labor force with thousands of men." For as long as Brezhnev was in power, Adylov was safe. He was not arrested until Gorbachev came to power and tried to clean up the massive mess Brezhnev and his associates had left behind.

THE END OF THE BREZHNEV ERA

Leonid Brezhnev died in late 1982. During his last years he was too sick to pay any attention to what was happening around him. His two immediate successors, both sick elderly men, between them governed for less than three years. Finally, in March 1985, Mikhail Gorbachev became the Soviet leader. His attempts to reform the Soviet system at first impressed many observers and raised hopes, at least in some quarters, that it could be mended. Instead, it soon became clear that the rot was so extensive and deep that efforts to fix the system were causing it to collapse. Like the rest of the Soviet Union, Central Asia was about to be swept up in unexpected change its Communist bosses, who once seemed so powerful, were unable to control.

NOTES

p. 47 "'From now on your beliefs . . .'" Quoted in Svat Soucek, *A History of Inner Asia* (Cambridge, England: Cambridge University Press, 2000), p. 211.

p. 54 "When the Communist shock troops began to . . ." Quoted in Michael Rywkin, *Moscow's Muslim Challenge: Soviet Central Asia*, revised edition (Armonk: M.E. Sharpe, 1990), p. 45.

p. 61 "'not only dozens of Japanese tea sets . . .'" David Remnik, *Lenin's Tomb: The Last Days of the Soviet Empire* (New York: Random House, 1993), p. 189.

p. 62 "'on a vast estate with peacocks . . .'" Remnik, *Lenin's Tomb: The Last Days of the Soviet Empire*, p. 186

5

REFORM, COLLAPSE, AND INDEPENDENCE

Mikhail Gorbachev was a career Communist Party politician who worked his way up through the ranks before being chosen general secretary, or party leader, in March 1985. When he took office many top party leaders believed that the Soviet Union had to undertake major reforms. The Soviet economy was stagnant. Even its ordinary citizens were increasingly aware of how far their standard of living lagged behind that of the democratic countries of the West. The Soviet Union, despite more than a half century of trying to make the collective farm system work, could not feed itself. It had become the world's largest importer of wheat. Economic problems and outdated technology in many industries meant that the Soviet Union could not match the modern military weapons of its superpower rival, the United States. Corruption was both draining valuable resources into an uncontrollable black market economy and demoralizing the population. Alcohol abuse, a problem in Russia long before 1917, and drug abuse—a new problem—were taking a toll on the health of the country. There was unrest among the Soviet Union's non-Russian nationalities, although the secret police and other organs of repression kept it from getting out of hand. Growing material inequality in a society supposedly based on socialist ideals had created widespread cynicism among the population. As the saying went, "We have communism, but not for everybody." Cynicism was evident even in the higher ranks of the party, among the very people who received the best and the most of what the Soviet Union had to offer.

These were only some of the problems Mikhail Gorbachev and his supporters had to solve. That situation was bad, and the obstacles to change were formidable. Because of the secrecy that pervaded Soviet society, not even its leaders knew how bad things were. Officials at all levels of government and administration commonly falsified reports. Lying was both a routine practice and an art form. Information that Soviet planners received was so unreliable that they often turned to the American Central Intelligence Agency's estimates of their country's output. Just as serious, many officials at every level of the Communist Party hierarchy opposed meaningful reform because it might threaten their positions and privileges.

Finally, when Gorbachev began his reform program, which he called *perestroika*, or "restructuring," he soon found that the limited changes he had in mind were not enough to do the job. For example, Gorbachev wanted to relax censorship under a policy he called *glasnost*, or "openness." He hoped that a freer flow of information would help expose corruption and energize a range of reform efforts. Glasnost also would help close the country's technological gap with the West by giving scientists access to information from abroad. Yet Gorbachev, as the head of the Communist Party, faced a contradiction. He did not want to see glasnost go too far. He still wanted the Communist Party leaders like himself to decide how much the people should know. Glasnost, in short, would be strictly limited.

The same contradiction plagued political reforms. By 1987 Gorbachev had decided the Soviet Union had to become more democratic. But he did not want democracy as that idea is understood in the West. Instead, at least at first, he wanted the Communist Party to remain the only political party in the Soviet Union. Reforms would be limited to how the party selected its officials and leaders. On the economic front, Gorbachev wanted to reform the Soviet Union's centrally planned economy, including the collective farm system. He did not want to dismantle it and replace it with a free market system, the economic system that in the West had proved so much more efficient than the Soviet Union's socialist system. Yet meaningful change required moving in that direction.

What happened was that a little glasnost immediately brought demands for more and, in fact, an abolition of *all* censorship. Plans to democratize the Communist Party led to runaway criticism of the party and demands for genuine multiparty democracy. Tinkering with the economy did not improve it, but caused it to sputter even more. When Gorbachev responded by introducing more extensive reforms, they began to undermine the very economy and the Communist institutions that held the Soviet Union together. By 1989, the process of change was speeding up and bursting beyond Gorbachev's desperate attempts to keep it under control. Restructuring had inadvertently become deconstruction. By 1991, chaos had replaced change and the Soviet Union had collapsed, leaving the Russians and the 14 minority nationalities of the non-Russian former union republics of the Soviet Union on their own as independent nations. Of all those republics, the ones least prepared for that challenge were the five Muslim republics of Central Asia.

Perestroika in Central Asia

Perestroika in Central Asia began with anticorruption campaigns that included leadership changes in the local Communist organizations. The main results were an upsurge in nationalist and ethnic consciousness, measures to elevate the status of local languages, and several serious ethnic clashes that left hundreds of people dead and thousands injured.

In Kazakhstan, Gorbachev attempted to clean up local corruption by replacing local party boss Dinmukhamed Kunayev with an ethnic Russian named Gennadi Kolbin. He took that step in December 1986. Seeing a fellow Kazakh replaced by a Russian from Moscow hit a raw nerve in the Kazakh community, which expected that the local Communist boss would be one of them. The response shocked Moscow. Demonstrations in Alma Ata turned into riots. Before the army could restore order, more than 200 people were killed and thousands more injured and arrested. Kolbin's efforts to clean up corruption and make other reforms then ran up against a clannish wall of local resistance. In 1989, Moscow gave up and recalled Kolbin. His replacement, Nursultan Nazarbayev, was a party official with a reputation for competence.

Meanwhile, by 1989 the Communist Party dictatorship that had once kept tight control over the Soviet Union had become badly frayed, and keeping order was becoming more difficult. This was reflected in ethnic violence, which in Kazakhstan took the form of attacks by unemployed Kazakh youths on members of a small minority group called the Lezghins. The Kazakhs accused the Lezghins and other immigrant workers of taking their jobs and demanded that they be expelled from Kazakhstan. The attacks resulted in five people killed, more than 100 people injured, and more than 3,500 people fleeing their homes. At the same time, Kazakh nationalist feeling was crystallizing beyond the point where even respected local Communist leaders like Nazarbayev could control it. He was unable to stop the normally powerless local Kazakh parliament, for example, from passing a resolution calling for Kazakh to become the official language of the Kazakh SSR.

The pattern in Kazakhstan was repeated elsewhere with local variations. In Uzbekistan, the cotton scam of the Brezhnev era was exposed. This led to the removal of several high-ranking officials and a series of corruption trials. The Uzbek response on the street was anger, arising from a belief that Uzbekistan had been unfairly singled out for punishment. Meanwhile, the loosening of central controls allowed long-simmering ethnic tensions to explode into violence. In June of 1989, Uzbek mobs in the Fergana Valley attacked people from the minority Meskhetian Turk community, leaving more than 100 people dead. In 1989, Islam Karimov, who in 1990 became the country's president, was appointed Communist Party leader in Uzbekistan. Meanwhile, Central Asia's first signs of thoughtful political opposition emerged when Uzbek intellectuals formed several organizations with nationalist agendas. The first, founded in Tashkent in November 1988, was a group called Birlik (Unity). Its issues included the need to diversify Uzbekistan's agriculture to grow less cotton and more food crops, to stem the drying up of the Aral Sea, and to elevate the status of the Uzbek language. In October 1989, the Uzbek parliament acted on the language issue by declaring Uzbek to be Uzbekistan's official language.

Kyrgyzstan watched these developments, but did not follow exactly in the footsteps of its neighbors. Pushed by the pressures of perestroika, the local Kyrgyz Communist Party chief retired late in 1985. However, his successor, Absamat Masaliyev, did little to support Gorbachev and perestroika, siding instead with critics in Moscow who argued that reforms were undermining the Soviet system. The freer atmosphere gave rise to new expressions of Kyrgyz nationalist sentiment, as well as more open

Aksar Akayev began his political career during the late Soviet era as a reformer, but has become increasingly authoritarian as president of independent Kyrgyzstan. (Courtesy Embassy of the Kyrgyz Republic, Washington, D.C.)

observance of Islam, not only by ordinary people, but by party workers and officials. In September 1989, the local Kyrgyz parliament declared Kyrgyz the republic's official language. Like other Central Asian republics, Kyrgyzstan had its own simmering ethnic conflict. The republic was about 13 percent Uzbek. Most Uzbeks lived in and around Osh, a city in the Fergana Valley very close to the Uzbek border. In June 1990, a land dispute between the Kyrgyz-dominated Osh city council and an Uzbek collective farm led to bloody riots in which at least 300 people died before Soviet troops restored order.

Kyrgyzstan took a slightly different path from the other Central Asian republics in two respects. In May 1990, a multiethnic umbrella organization was formed called Democratic Kyrgyzstan. Made up of 24 Kyrgyz and Russian groups favoring democratic reform, it soon had a membership of more than 100,000. Democratic Kyrgyzstan enhanced its popular standing during June when it helped calm disturbances related to the Osh riots in Frunze, the republic's capital. Four months later, in October, Democratic Kyrgyzstan played an important role in influencing the Kyrgyz parliament's choice of a person to fill the newly created office of president of the Kyrgyz SSR. The establishment of the new office was not unusual; other union republics throughout the Soviet Union were doing the same thing. They were following the example set by Gorbachev in March when he convinced the Soviet parliament to create a new powerful presidency of the Soviet Union and then elect him to that post. What was different in Kyrgyzstan was that the successful candidate was not the local party boss, Absamat Masaliyev, but a physicist and former head of the Kyrgyz Academy of Sciences named Askar Akayev. What also made Akayev different, especially in Central Asia, was that he was genuinely committed to reform.

In Tajikistan, corruption, the language issue, ethnic tension, and religion dominated the post-1985 era. In 1985 Gorbachev forced the incumbent Tajik Communist Party leader, a corrupt Brezhnev-era holdover named Rahmon Nabiyev, from office. Nabiyev departed along with many of his equally corrupt colleagues. His replacement, Kakhar Mahkamov, although hardly a committed reformer, followed Moscow's example by easing censorship and permitting more freedom of expression. The status of the Tajik language then immediately became a major public issue, and in 1989 the Tajik parliament voted to make Tajik the official religion of the republic. During the summer of that year Tajikistan's ethnic problems surfaced when serious fighting over land broke out between Tajiks and Uzbeks. In February 1990, there were massive riots in the capital of Dushanbe in response to a rumor that Armenian refugees from Azerbaijan would be resettled in the city and given priority access to scarce jobs and housing. It took more than 5,000 Soviet troops to restore order, which only came after a reported 22 deaths and 565 injuries.

Perhaps most significant for the long-term future of Tajikistan was the emergence of Islamic fundamentalism. By 1989, Islamic activists were anonymously distributing leaflets that urged parents to educate their children according to Islamic law. Young girls were the first target. They were pressured to give up their secular European ways, including their style of dress. Some fathers began keeping their daughters home from school or forcing them to marry against their will. A newly organized fundamentalist group called the Islamic Renaissance Party began to draw popular support, even though it was denied the right to hold a founding congress.

Perestroika had the least impact in Turkmenistan. In 1985 the republic got a new party leader, Saparmurat Niyazov, a career politician who had little use for reform. Yet by 1987, even in Turkmenistan intellectuals and some politicians were complaining about the status of the Turkmen language, the environmental impact of Soviet economic policies on the countryside, and the general economic exploitation of Turkmenistan by the Soviet government.

The Soviet Collapse and Unwanted Independence

By 1990 the bonds holding the Soviet Union together clearly were weakening. However, Central Asia's five main non-Russian nationalities were not seeking independence. Several factors account for this attitude, which set the Central Asians apart from a number of European non-Russian nationalities. None of the main Central Asian ethnic groups had a history of independence as nation states. The party leaders and the huge number of bureaucrats who managed the union republics owed their positions and relatively comfortable life styles to the Soviet system and feared they would lose everything if the system collapsed. Many were Russified to a significant degree and more comfortable speaking Russian than the native language of their republics. It was also true that despite Moscow's exploitation of the region, Central Asia made considerable material progress during the Soviet era. Educational, social, and economic conditions were far better than those in the Muslim countries to the south or in the Middle East. Literacy was almost universal in Soviet Central Asia, and women enjoyed freedoms well beyond what their sisters had in traditional Muslim societies outside the Soviet Union. In Kazakhstan, Nazarbayev and other leaders were concerned with their republic's territorial integrity. In particular, they worried that any move toward independence would incite ethnic Russians, who made up the majority in many parts of the north, to secede and become part of Russia.

To be sure, some intellectuals and educated professionals wanted independence, but they were a tiny, if articulate, percentage of the population. In the Baltic republics of Lithuania, Latvia, and Estonia, the dream of independence became a reality after a decades-long struggle. In Central Asia, independence that few had asked for, or even wanted, came suddenly and almost without warning.

During 1990 and 1991, Central Asia was pulled toward independence as the Soviet Union careened toward collapse. During 1990, every union republic in the region established a new and powerful post of president. The elections of the new presidents in Central Asia, conducted between March and November, had more in common with Soviet practice than with Western balloting. Of the five successful candidates, four—Uzbekistan's Karimov, Kazakhstan's Nazarbayev, Turkmenistan's Niyazov, and Tajikistan's Mahkamov—were the current party leaders. The only exception was Kyrgyzstan's Akayev. All with the exception of Turkmenistan's Niyazov were elected by their respective Communist-dominated parliaments. Niyazov allowed the population to vote in an election in which, like the Communist boss he was, he ran unopposed. Not surprisingly, he won with a whopping 98.3 percent of the vote. These elections had long-term implications. Four of the new presidents—Nazarbayev in Kazakhstan, Niyazov in Turkmenistan, Karimov in Uzbekistan, and Akayev in Kyrgyzstan—would remain president when their republics became independent countries in 1991.

While the presidential elections were going on, the parliaments of the union republics throughout the Soviet Union were declaring what they called sovereignty. Exactly what this term meant in the Soviet Union during 1990 was not clear. Different parliaments certainly had different things in mind when they used the term, but at a minimum it implied greater control over local affairs. In Central Asia, the declarations of sovereignty clearly were more limited in intent than in other parts of the Soviet Union. This was demonstrated in a referendum Gorbachev sponsored in March 1991. Soviet voters were asked whether they wanted to see the Soviet Union preserved "as a renewed federation of equal sovereign republics, in which the rights and freedom of an individual of any nationality will be fully guaranteed." Six republics refused to participate, mainly out of a desire to secure independence. Of the nine that did participate, 76.4 voted to preserve the reformed union. The greatest support for the continued union came from Central Asia, where approval rates ranged as high as 94 percent in Kazakhstan and 95.7 percent in Turkmenistan. No doubt these results were heavily influenced by the local ruling elite, but they also indicated a widespread conservatism and reluctance to dismantle the Soviet Union.

This outlook was reaffirmed in early August 1991, when Communist Party hard-liners in Moscow attempted to overthrow Gorbachev. Their goal was to reverse his reforms and, as far as possible, restore the Soviet Union to its pre-1985 form. Only Kyrgyzstan's Askar Akayev immediately came out against the coup. Akayev had an incentive, however: Party leaders in Kyrgyzstan who supported the Moscow hard-liners were planning a coup of their own in Kyrgyzstan. Kazakhstan's Nazarbayev, the only other regional president with reformist credentials, did not announce his opposition to the coup until the second day, when it already was in trouble and about to fail. The presidents of Tajikistan and Turkmenistan did not oppose the coup, while in Uzbekistan, President Karimov, who made no public statements when it mattered, may well have been in contact with the coup plotters.

In any event, the coup unleashed a chain reaction that doomed the Soviet Union. Every union republic declared its independence, including the Central Asian republics, which were the last to take the plunge. Kyrgyzstan and, ironically, Uzbekistan, both of which declared independence on August 31, led Central Asia into the realm of independence. Tajikistan followed suit in September and Turkmenistan in October. The last of all the Soviet republics to act was Kazakhstan, which declared its independence on December 16. A few days later, the five Central Asian republics joined with six others in the Kazakh capital of Almaty to sign a declaration establishing the Commonwealth of Independent States (CIS), a loose association lacking any authority or clear definition or function. The declaration that established the CIS also declared the Soviet Union abolished. On December 25, Mikhail Gorbachev resigned as president of what in reality was already a nonexistent Soviet Union. Official end came on midnight of December 31, 1991. The five former Soviet republics in Central Asia were independent states, on their own, and burdened with enormous problems they were ill-prepared to solve.

NOTE

p. 71 "'as a renewed federation . . .'" Richard Sakwa, *The Rise and Fall of the Soviet Union, 1917–1991* (London and New York: Routledge, 1999), p. 472.

6

INDEPENDENT CENTRAL ASIA

When the states of Central Asia became independent in the waning days of 1991, each faced its own difficult circumstances. At the same time, certain serious problems were common to all of them. These included authoritarian political traditions, failing economies, widespread crime and corruption, and an upsurge of Islamic fundamentalism. The origins of these conditions were diverse. Some were rooted in Central Asian history that reached back centuries, others in the seven decades spent as part of the Soviet Union, and yet others in both legacies.

Political Conditions

Central Asian political life showed distinct similarities from country to country. Between 1992 and 1996, all of the Central Asian states adopted new constitutions that included the guarantees of political and human rights associated with Western democracies. But neither these constitutions nor their guarantees in reality meant very much. All the newly independent Central Asian states inherited their political leadership, key institutions, and habits of operation from the Soviet era. All of their presidents at the time of independence were former Communist Party bosses or, in the case of Kyrgyzstan's Akayev, first came to power by being elected by a Communist-dominated parliament. Beneath them, former Communist bureaucrats occupied seats in post-Soviet parliaments and staffed government offices. Clan and regional connections, essential to the local way of life centuries before the Russians arrived, remained crucial to getting things done. Official corruption, well entrenched during the Soviet era, grew even worse.

SULTANISTIC REGIMES

The dominant trend throughout Central Asia over the next decade was toward one-man dictatorial rule. The common pattern resembled what some political scientists have called sultanistic regimes: dictatorships in which loyalty to the ruler is not based on a political program or ideology, or on any outstanding qualities the ruler may have. Instead, loyalty and service are based on fear and the rewards the ruler supplies to his supporters. The sultanistic regimes that emerged in Central Asia during the 1990s were not new. Rather, they were a return to an authoritarian Central Asian tradition that long antedated Russian or Soviet control.

The exception to strong one-man rule was Tajikistan, but not because of political pluralism or anything having to do with democracy, progress, or stability. Rather, between 1992 and 1997, Tajikistan was torn by civil war between the former Communist establishment and Islamic fundamentalists.

THE RUSSIAN PRESENCE IN INDEPENDENT CENTRAL ASIA

Russian influence was another common political reality in newly independent Central Asia, especially in Kazakhstan and Tajikistan. This had little to do with the formal existence of the Commonwealth of Independent States (CIS), to which all the Central Asian countries belonged, because the CIS had no authority over its members. What mattered was Russian economic influence over the local economies, Moscow's military power, and the presence of Russian communities that included many people with essential technical and managerial skills. From the start Tajikistan was in reality nothing more than a Russian protectorate. Between

1992 and 1997, Russian troops played a vital role in supporting Tajikistan's government of former Soviet politicians in a civil war and preventing Islamic forces from taking over the country. After the civil war, most Russian troops stayed, both to back up the government at home and to prevent militant Islamic armed groups from crossing Tajikistan's southern border with war-torn Afghanistan.

Russia's formal military ties to other Central Asian states consisted mainly of an agreement called the CIS Collective Security Treaty (CST). This Russian-sponsored agreement was signed in 1992 by Russia and eight other CIS members, among them all the Central Asian states except Turkmenistan. However, throughout the 1990s the treaty led to little actual cooperation.

Russian demographic influence in Central Asia in 1992 was greatest in Kazakhstan, where ethnic Russians made up about 38 percent of the total population, only a few percentage points less than the Kazakh total of 40 percent. In fact, Russians and Ukrainians (5 percent) together outnumbered the Kazakhs in Kazakhstan, although Russian/Ukrainian emigration and a high Kazakh birthrate soon reversed that relationship. The Russian community also carried considerable weight in Kyrgyzstan, where at independence Russians made up about 21 percent of the population. (In 1992, Russians made up about 8 percent of the population in Uzbekistan and Tajikistan and about 9 percent in Turkmenistan.) However, emigration sharply reduced all these figures over the next 10 years, and with them the influence of these Russian communities. Still, as of 2002 Russians still were either the largest (in Kazakhstan and Uzbekistan) or second largest (in Kyrgyzstan, Tajikistan, and Turkmenistan) minority in every Central Asian country.

During Central Asia's first decade of independence, Russian influence in the region declined in other ways, most noticeable in Uzbekistan and Turkmenistan. Turkmenistan almost immediately announced it would be neutral in world affairs and refused to cooperate with Russian efforts to stabilize the government of Tajikistan. In Uzbekistan, the government actively tried to downplay the Russian-Soviet role in the country's history. At the same time, Uzbekistan sometimes actively competed with Russia for influence in the four other Central Asian states. In 1999, Uzbekistan withdrew from the Collective Security Treaty. That and other withdrawals left only six members in the CST, including Russia,

Kazakhstan, Tajikistan, and Kyrgyzstan. Russia's predominance in Central Asia was further reduced after radical Islamic Arab terrorists destroyed the World Trade Center in New York City on September 11, 2001. That act brought the United States into Central Asia. The terrorists belonged to an organization called al-Qaeda. It was based in Afghanistan and protected by that country's radical Islamic government, known as the Taliban. As part of its military campaign to destroy the Taliban and al-Qaeda in Afghanistan, the United States signed agreements with Uzbekistan and Kyrgyzstan permitting the United States to set up military bases in those countries. Russia's response came about a year later. In December 2002, it signed a security agreement with Kyrgyzstan calling for a Russian airbase in that country. The new Russian base, in northern Kyrgyzstan near Bishkek, was built about 40 miles (60 km) from the U.S. base. Along with plans for a ground force composed of troops from Russia, Kazakhstan, Tajikistan, and Kyrgyzstan, the new air base was generally viewed as Russia's attempt to reassert its presence in Central Asia and make the CST a treaty with real meaning.

THE CENTRAL ASIAN NUCLEAR-WEAPON-FREE ZONE

On September 27, 2002, after five years of negotiations, the five states of Central Asia took a decisive step forward by agreeing to a treaty making their region a nuclear-weapon-free zone. The Central Asian nuclear-weapon-free zone was the world's fifth, and the first in the Northern Hemisphere. Although no Central Asian state was a candidate to develop nuclear weapons, the treaty was important for several reasons. First, prior to its collapse, the Soviet Union had kept nuclear weapons in the region. Kazakhstan, in fact, briefly became a nuclear power when it inherited more than 1,300 Soviet nuclear weapons in 1991. It voluntarily gave up these weapons by 1995. Second, Central Asia bordered on two nuclear weapons powers, Russia and China, as well as on two unstable regions, the Middle East and South Asia, where several countries either had or were seeking to develop nuclear weapons. Furthermore, the treaty provided an example of regional cooperation that was badly needed in a part of the world with so many problems and few success stories after more than a decade of independence.

Economic and Social Problems

The Soviet Union's centrally planned economy had been unraveling for years before the entire political system fell apart in late 1991. Economic decline continued for the next decade. Under the Soviet system of planned integration, each region had played an assigned role in the country's overall economy. That role was determined in Moscow, usually without regard for local welfare. Although there had been significant industrial development in Central Asia during the Soviet era, for the most part a predominately colonial relationship had prevailed between the region and the European parts of the Soviet Union. Central Asia provided raw materials, such as cotton, wheat, or minerals, in return for industrial goods. Central Asian factories depended on other parts of the Soviet Union for vital supplies and customers for their goods. After independence vital suppliers suddenly lay beyond international borders, making it far more complicated and often much more expensive to do business with them. Major customers, if they continued to exist at all in other parts of the former Soviet Union, were now in foreign countries, in the majority of cases in Russia but also countries like Ukraine or other former Soviet republics. Many Central Asian factories had supplied the huge Soviet military-industrial complex. Those orders dried up as the post-Soviet Russian military shrank drastically in both size and budget. Central Asia had depended on economic subsidies and other aid from Moscow. These subsidies funded education, medical care, pensions, and other vital social services. As 1991 ended and 1992 began, those subsidies disappeared. Along with them went many European residents, mainly Russians and Ukrainians, who decided to emigrate. Their departure deprived the vulnerable Central Asian economies of skilled factory workers and a large percentage of their technical and managerial personnel.

Central Asia was physically isolated from non-Soviet customers. That isolation was made worse by Soviet transportation networks. Only one railroad led to a destination other than Russia: It led into northern China, a lightly populated region with few customers or suppliers. In the West, there certainly were customers for Central Asian oil and gas, tens of millions of them in fact, but no pipelines to carry those valuable energy resources there. All Soviet-era pipelines led northward into Russia. Electricity grids and roads also tied the countries of Central Asia to Russia and other parts of the former Soviet Union.

In addition, the newly independent Central Asian states had to dismantle their inefficient socialist economies and make the difficult transition to free market economies. That task required what is called privatization: transferring state-owned factories, farms, and businesses to private ownership. It also required passing laws that make it possible for free markets to work. Yet most countries the local leadership inherited from the Soviet era showed little or no interest in undertaking that difficult transition.

Meanwhile, crime surged as tight Soviet controls disappeared. Much of that crime was associated with drug trafficking through poorly policed Central Asian borders into Russia and from there to markets in European countries further west. The problem in Central Asia grew more serious in the 1990s. By the year 2000, United Nations experts estimated that 80 percent of Europe's heroin originated in Afghanistan and Pakistan. Most of it began its journey to the West by crossing Kyrgyzstan, Tajikistan, and Kazakhstan. As the heroin passed through these countries of poor and rootless people, it picked up users, who in turn became addicts. Because the heroin so close to its source was cheap—an average dose in 2000 cost 50 cents in Tajikistan and $2 further north in Kyrgyzstan—it replaced opium, a weaker and less addictive narcotic, as the drug of choice in Central Asia. And with heroin addiction came H.I.V. infection and AIDS, which spread as addicts shared the needles they used to inject their drugs. It all added up to an expanding social tragedy and health crisis in countries without the resources to respond effectively.

Islamic Fundamentalism

One of the many failures of the Soviet attempt to remake humanity in a utopian communist image was its unsuccessful effort to suppress religion. Soviet campaigns to suppress Islam in Central Asia, which mirrored anti-religious campaigns elsewhere in the country, dated from the 1920s. They intensified during the 1930s, moderated during World War II, and intensified again—though not to the murderous level under Stalin during the 1930s—in the late 1950s and early 1960s. These campaigns and other anti-religious propaganda had an impact. They helped create a secularized and educated local elite who played a vital role in governing Central Asia and running its modern educational and economic institutions. But the Soviet regime could not eliminate the practice of Islam. Rather, repression drove it underground. Muslim rites were observed secretly, at times even by party officials.

When Soviet policy finally became more tolerant during the Gorbachev era, Islam revived immediately in Central Asia. Although this revival took Soviet officials in Moscow unawares, it should not have been such a surprise. Islam was the logical way for Central Asians to reconnect with their pre-Soviet historical and cultural identities, and they took advantage of their new freedoms under perestroika to do just that. In Central Asia, Western secular culture and democracy had little appeal, but religion did. By 1991, thousands of new mosques had been opened throughout the region, old shrines had been restored, and a revival that increased in depth and breadth after independence was well under way.

The Islamic revival that began in the 1980s had more than a spiritual side. There also was a political side, and it threatened to replace a secular tyranny with a religious one. A prominent journalist and leading authority on Islam in Central Asia writing in the year 2000 observed that "Islamic militancy remains the most potent threat to the five Central Asian Republics." The journalist was describing a movement that became a major force throughout the Muslim world during the last quarter of the 20th century, from the Middle East to Southeast Asia. Islamic militancy (also often called Muslim fundamentalism) in the 20th and 21st centuries is a reaction to Western power and influence. It is a militant rejection of Western secular ideas and values by Muslims who see those values as a threat to the Islamic way of life. Muslim fundamentalists consider most of the regimes in the Muslim world, including those in Central Asia, to be insufficiently Islamic. They want to overthrow and replace them with regimes that govern according the *sharia*, or Islamic law. They actively support jihad, or holy war, which is the traditional Muslim military struggle to bring the entire world under the rule of Islamic law. Islamic fundamentalist groups have frequently resorted to terrorism and other forms of violence to accomplish their aims.

To a degree, Muslim fundamentalism in Central Asia was inconsistent with how Islam is practiced in the region. In large parts of Central Asia, particularly among the nomadic Kazakh, Kyrgyz, and Turkmen tribes, Islam often has been less restrictive and more tolerant than elsewhere in

New mosques filled with worshipers are an increasingly important part of daily life in Central Asia. Here, in October 2001, a Muslim religious leader, or mullah, delivers his sermon before prayers in the southern Uzbek town of Termez.
(AP/Wide World Photos/Efrem Lukatsky)

the Muslim world. This moderate tendency was most pronounced among the nomads of the Kazakh steppe, who were not completely converted to Islam until the 18th century. This observance of Islam incorporated pre-Muslim shamanistic and mystical practices that were a part of their nomadic way of life many centuries before they adopted Islam. These influences made the Kazakh form of worship and religious outlook far less rigid than it was in the cities of Uzbekistan or parts of southern Kyrgyzstan, where traditional mosques and Islamic schools dominated religious life. As a result, in the late 20th century the Kazakh nomads, as well as many Kyrgyz and Turkmen groups, were far less likely to be influenced by militant Islamic doctrines infiltrating into Central Asia than, for example, their Uzbek, Tajik, or Kyrgyz coreligionists in southern oasis regions such as the Fergana Valley.

These latter areas, however, presented a very different situation. With their more traditional forms of Islam and their severe economic and social problems, they contained many young people who provided a ready audience for militant and fundamentalist Islamic doctrines.

Outside influences played a central role in turning part of Central Asia's Islamic revival in the direction of Muslim fundamentalism. One outside source was Afghanistan, where Muslim guerrillas, often with extreme fundamentalist views, fought a Soviet occupation army supporting an unpopular local Communist regime from 1979 until the Soviets withdrew in 1988. Some of the Soviet soldiers were young Central Asian draftees. By sending them to Afghanistan, the Soviet government unintentionally exposed its citizens to the wider Muslim world and fundamentalist ideas. It was not unusual for Central Asian soldiers taken prisoner by the Afghan guerrillas to switch sides and, when they eventually returned home, to spread their fundamentalist ideas to other young people. By the late 1980s, hundreds of young Uzbeks and Tajiks from Soviet Central Asia secretly were studying in Islamic schools called *madrasas* in Pakistan and Saudi Arabia. There they were indoctrinated with fundamentalist ideas and often trained to become guerrilla fighters in the cause of militant Islam.

The role of Saudi Arabia is of special importance in the spread of Islamic fundamentalism. Since the 1970s, Saudi Arabia had been using its enormous oil wealth to spread its version of Islamic fundamentalism. Called Wahhabism, it is a militant, intolerant creed hostile to the West, Christianity and Judaism, and virtually anything that does not fit the strict and austere Wahhabi definition of Islam. Saudi money went to Afghanistan, to fundamentalist *madrasas* throughout Pakistan, and eventually to Central Asia to promote the Wahhabi creed there. Many of the preachers spreading Wahhabi doctrines in Central Asia by the 1990s were trained in *madrasas* in Saudi Arabia or Saudi-funded schools in Pakistan.

By independence, Islamic fundamentalist groups were well established in several Central Asian countries. The most important and wide-spread was the Islamic Renaissance Party (IRP). The IRP did not get its start in Central Asia. It was founded in 1990 in the Russian city of Astrakhan by local Muslim intellectuals. It then spread and soon had a secret branch in Tajikistan. When that branch emerged from underground and officially registered as a legal Tajik political party in December 1991, it claimed 20,000 members. The IRP also established a large following in Uzbekistan, in particular in the Fergana Valley, but had to remain underground there because of the repression by the Uzbek government. The organization also took route in Kyrgyzstan, but only in the southern part of the country among its Uzbek minority. It had less success in the rest of

Kyrgyzstan, in Kazakhstan, and in Turkmenistan. Over time the IRP suffered a series of internal disputes and lost support outside Tajikistan.

By then, however, other Islamic fundamentalist groups had emerged and gained strength. They remain an important part of Central Asian religious and political life. The most important as of the beginning of 2003 are the Islamic Movement of Uzbekistan (IMU) and Hizb-ut-Tahrir al-Islami (HT; Party of Islamic Liberation), a group founded in the Middle East during the 1950s. These militant and intolerant groups are major players in the struggle to shape the future of Central Asia. Whatever their disagreements, collectively they threaten the region's autocratic regimes and the far weaker groups who want to bring democracy to Central Asia.

NOTE

p. 79 "'Islamic militancy remains the most potent threat . . .'" Ahmed Rashid, "Confrontation Brews Among Islamic Militants in Central Asia." Central Asia Caucasus Analyst, Weekly Briefing. November 22, 2000. Available on-line. URL:http://cacianalnst.org/Nov_22_2000/Islamic_Militants_in_Central_Asia. htm. Downloaded August 18, 2002.

PART II
The Central Asian Republics Today

7

KAZAKHSTAN

When Kazakhstan became independent, it appeared to have the best overall prospects in Central Asia. Its political leadership, while inherited from the Soviet era and hardly democratic, seemed receptive to limited political and economic reform. Kazakhstan's leadership was less autocratic and more respected in international circles than the leadership of Uzbekistan, Turkmenistan, or Tajikistan. Despite serious problems with its economy, Kazakhstan had enormous economic potential, more than any other Central Asian state. Foreign investors were very interested in its oil and gas fields. There also was foreign interest in other valuable mineral deposits and even in some of Kazakhstan's factories. A skilled workforce awaited those investors. However, these prospects were not realized during Kazakhstan's first decade of independence, and many problems became worse. Some experts have blamed the disappointments of that decade on political leadership that lacked either the will or the vision to take advantage of real opportunities. Others have argued that Kazakhstan's economic and political problems outweighed its potential and dragged the country down. In particular, the absence of the tradition of the rule of law guaranteeing limited government and protecting property rights, a condition common to all of Central Asia, is viewed as a barrier that no foreign investment or aid could overcome. This is not a debate that can be easily settled. What can be said is that Kazakhstan's first decade of independence was a difficult one and that as a result it began the new century under trying circumstances.

A Country Map

Kazakhstan is a huge country, extending about 1,200 miles (1,931 km) from the Caspian Sea in the west to the Altai Mountains in the east, and about 800 miles (1,287 km) from the plains of Siberia in the north to Central Asia's parched deserts in the south. Shaped something like a huge tank rumbling westward, Kazakhstan is the ninth largest country in the world. Its size puts it in several exclusive clubs. It accounted for about 12 percent of the former Soviet Union and was the second largest of the former Soviet republics, trailing only Russia. Kazakhstan's total area—1,049,200 square miles (2,717,428 sq km)— makes it one of only nine countries in the world with an area of more than 1 million square miles. It is one of three countries—Russia and Turkey are the other two—with territory in both Asia and Europe. Kazakhstan also is by far the planet's largest landlocked country. It is twice the size of all the other Central Asian countries combined, almost four times the size of Texas, and about equal in area to all of Western Europe.

Despite its great size and inland location, Kazakhstan borders on only five countries. To the north is Russia, whose vast territory also fronts on Kazakhstan's in the northwest. Kazakhstan's total border with Russia twists, turns, and undulates for 4,253 miles (6,843 km). It is one of the longest borders in the world, more than 250 miles longer than the United States–Canadian border that bisects the North American continent. South of the Russian border, the rest of Kazakhstan's western frontier is its jagged 1,176-mile (1,892-km) Caspian Sea coastline. Kazakhstan's eastern neighbor, across another long border, this one stretching for more than 952 miles (1,532 km), is China. In the south, running west to east, Kazakhstan's relatively short border (235 miles, 378 km) with Turkmen- istan gives way to the 1,368-mile (2,201-km) border with Uzbekistan, part of which crosses the dying Aral Sea on a diagonal from northwest to southeast. The Kazakhstan-Uzbekistan frontier feeds into Kazakhstan's 653-mile (1,051-km) border with Krygyzstan. These lengthy frontiers, in a region plagued by political instability and growing drug trafficking, often run through remote and inhospitable terrain and are impossible to police and effectively control, especially given Kazakhstan's limited resources.

Most of Kazakhstan is a plain averaging between 650 and 950 feet (200–300 m) above sea level that rises in elevation from west to east. Its western fringe, along the shore of the Caspian Sea—an area called the Caspian Depression—is below sea level, dipping to about 432 feet (132 m) below sea level at its lowest point. The plain's flat landscape is broken slightly by a hilly region in the west that is the southernmost appendix of Russia's Ural Mountains, and a larger and considerably higher hilly area in the center known as the Kazakh Hills. Kazakhstan's southeast and east are fringed by mountains: the northern slopes of the Tien Shan in the southeast along the border with Kyrgyzstan and the Altai Mountains in the country's extreme eastern corner where it meets China. The country's highest point is in the Tien Shan range, where snow-capped Mt. Khan Tengri towers almost 23,000 feet (7,000 m) above sea level as it straddles the Kazakh-Kyrgyz border.

The northern and western sections of the Kazakhstan plain consist primarily of a treeless grassland, or prairie. Large stretches of it were turned into farmland for growing wheat during the Soviet era. The central and southern sections, amounting to three-quarters of the entire country, are either semidesert or desert. They include a stony desert on a plateau between the Aral and Caspian Seas, and Kazakhstan's part of the Qizilqum (Red Sands) Desert, which it shares with Uzbekistan. Another of Kazakhstan's deserts, the Betbakdala clay desert, stretches eastward from the Aral Sea for more than 500 miles to Lake Balqash, Kazakhstan's largest lake and the largest body of water that lies entirely within the country. Further south, yet other desert regions dominate the landscape until the plains finally give way to mountains.

Kazakhstan's largest city is Almaty, its capital until 1997. It has a population of about 1.1 million and is located in the extreme southwestern part of the country. Its remote location was one reason the capital was moved to Aqmola, renamed Astana ("capital city" in Kazakh) in 1998, in the north-central part of the country. The newly built capital currently has a population of about 313,000. Other important cities include the industrial centers Karaganda (population: 437,000), Chimkent (population: 360,000), Pavlodar (population: 300,000) and Semey (population: 270,000). During the 1990s, more than 2 million citizens of Kazakhstan moved from rural areas to the cities, raising the percentage of the population living in urban areas above 60 percent. That mass movement has led to urban decay and other problems in many cities, as there are not enough jobs or housing for the new arrivals, almost all of whom are poor and without the skills needed to find good jobs.

LAKES AND RIVERS IN A DRY LAND

Lake Balqash, in eastern Kazakhstan, is one of the world's more unusual lakes. Like Kazakhstan itself, the lake is landlocked, lacking an outlet. About 376 miles (605 km) long and 45 miles (72 km) wide, it covers an area of about 7,115 square miles (18,428 sq km), making it Asia's fourth-largest lake in area and the 16th largest in the world. It is, however, very shallow, averaging about 20 feet (6 m) in depth and reaching a maximum depth of only 87 feet (26 m). At one point on the eastern end of the lake, the sandy bottom drops off so gradually that a person of average height can walk from the shore into the water for more than 1,000 yards. Lake Balqash is fed by three main rivers, the largest of which, flowing westward out of China, is the Ili River. Before entering Lake Balqash near its south-

Local residents depend on Lake Balqash for fish to eat and/or sell, but irrigation projects along rivers that feed the lake are depriving it of the water it needs to maintain its ecological balance. (AP Photo/Boris Buzin)

western tip, the Ili forms a large delta and wetland region featuring many lakes, marshes, and thick vegetation.

Lake Balqash is usually frozen from November to March during Kazakhstan's harsh winter. Its most unique feature is that it is in a sense two lakes in one: a salt lake in the east and a freshwater lake in the west, a condition caused by a sand bar that effectively divides the lake into two sections. The lake's fragile ecosystem is threatened by human activity. Its waters have been polluted by copper smelters built on its shores in the 1930s, although many species of fish manage to survive and even flourish. Irrigation increasingly has deprived the lake of water from the Ili and other rivers, with the result that its water level has been dropping since 1960. The greatest menace to the lake is China's plan to dam the Ili River. That scheme could kill Lake Balqash altogether, causing it to dry up like the Aral Sea and add to Central Asia's long list of ecological disasters. The proposed project also would deprive Kazakhstan of an annual supply of fish important to the country's food supply. The Ili River in fact already has a major dam on it about 200 miles from where it enters Lake Balqash; behind that dam is a 60-mile-long (100-km) reservoir whose cold, fresh waters have made it a popular local vacation destination. The best recent news about Lake Balqash was the Kazakh government's decision in 2000 to cancel plans to build a nuclear power plant along its shores. That decision came a year after the country's only nuclear power plant was shut down after almost 26 years of operation.

Kazakhstan has other salt lakes, the most important of which is Lake Tengiz. Located in the Kazakh Hills in the north-central part of the country, Lake Tengiz, 780 square miles (2,000 sq. km) in area, is near several smaller freshwater lakes and is the core of one of Kazakhstan's most important wetlands. The surrounding region is home to more than 300 species of birds including flamingos, cranes, eagles, and an endangered species of pelican, and more than 50 mammal species. It has been designated a nature reserve.

Aside from the Ili, Kazakhstan's two main rivers are the Syr Darya and the Irtysh. The Syr Darya enters Kazakhstan from Uzbekistan and then takes a northwesterly route to the Aral Sea. The Irtysh is the largest tributary of the Ob River, a major Siberian river that flows northward into the Arctic Sea. The Irtysh rises in the Altai Mountains in China and crosses the northeastern corner of Kazakhstan. There, still in the Altai

Mountains, it enters and then exits Lake Zaysan, a freshwater lake of about 700 square miles (1,813 sq km) rich in fish. The river then parallels the Kazakh-Russian border for about 600 miles (965 km) before crossing into Russia and linking up with the Ob. Along that route it first meets two tributaries that begin in Kazakhstan but likewise flow northward into Russia: the Tobol, which rises in northern Kazakhstan near the Russian border, and the Ishim, which rises in the north-central part of the country near its new capital, Astana.

The Irtysh is very important to Kazakhstan. It is the main source of water for several cities in the north and for more than 4 million people, about a quarter of the country's population. The river is vital to industry and hydroelectric power stations in the area and is central to government plans for the region's further development. A canal built during the 1960s brings Irtysh water to the industrial city of Karaganda in the central part of the country and also supports agricultural development in that region. The problem for Kazakhstan is that China plans to build a canal of its own to divert water for the development in arid northeast China. China claims it plans to divert only a tenth of the river's flow, which will presumably leave plenty of water for Kazakhstan. However, the Kazakh government is unconvinced by China's assurances. It has been discussing the matter with the Chinese since the late 1990s, but has been unable to get East Asia's rising superpower to modify its plans. Kazakhstan has little leverage with its powerful neighbor to the east. Aside from the huge discrepancy in power between the two countries, Kazakhstan needs China. In 1997, the two countries signed a $9 billion deal for a pipeline that will bring Kazakh oil to markets in China. Ironically, the pipeline Kazakhstan wants will pass near the canal it does not want, and the Chinese are very likely to insist that the two projects be linked. This means Kazakhstan will have to accept the loss of water, a resource in which it is seriously deficient, in order to sell oil, a resource of which it has far more than it needs and must sell in order to prosper economically.

NATURAL RESOURCES

Kazakhstan has plenty of natural resources. A Soviet geologist once stated that Kazakhstan could export the entire periodic table of elements. While that was all exaggeration, Kazakhstan does have many mineral resources. These include 90 percent of the former Soviet Union's chrome, almost half of its lead, copper, and zinc; and large deposits of manganese, tungsten, gold, silver, copper, and molybdenum. Kazakhstan also has large coal deposits. It was the Soviet Union's third-largest coal producer, trailing only Russia and the Ukraine, and today is the largest exporter of coal to the other former Soviet republics. Coal currently produces almost 45 percent of Kazakhstan's energy, as opposed to about 25 percent each by oil and natural gas. Kazakhstan also has large deposits of iron and the second-largest gold reserves in the world. Only about 12 percent of Kazakhstan is arable, but the country still has almost 100 million acres of farmland, most of which is used for growing wheat, and even vaster pastures for grazing livestock, mainly cattle and sheep. Kazakhstan also produces cotton and a variety of fruits and vegetables.

These plentiful resources all take second place to oil and natural gas, the two energy sources upon which the industrialized world increasingly depends. Kazakhstan currently has more than 70 trillion cubic feet of proven natural gas reserves, placing it among the world's top 20 potential suppliers of that clean-burning energy source. More important by far are Kazakhstan's oil reserves. Proven reserves currently are estimated by most experts to be about 17.6 billion barrels. However, Kazakhstan has many potentially oil-rich regions that have not yet been explored, and many experts believe the current figure could easily triple, enough to make Kazakhstan a leading oil producer and exporter. As the U.S. government's Energy Information Administration reported in July 2002, "Kazakhstan's possible hydrocarbon reserves, both onshore and offshore, dwarf its proven reserves, with estimated possible reserves—mostly in the Kazakh sector of the Caspian Sea—of between 30 billion and 50 billion barrels." That helps explain why foreign companies invested about $13 billion in Kazakhstan's oil and natural gas industries between 1991 and 2001. During that period, despite severe economic problems and general economic decline, Kazakhstan's oil production jumped from 530,000 to 810,000 barrels per day, and earnings from oil sales in 2000 topped $5 billion. Estimated output for 2002 was more than 900,000 barrels per day, while projections for 2015 were as high as 2.5 million barrels per day.

Most of the new production is expected to come from three gigantic fields. Two of them—Tengiz, just inland from the northern Caspian Sea shore, and Karachaganak, just south of the Russian border in western Kazakhstan—are currently being developed and have begun production. The Kashgan field, which lies offshore in the Caspian Sea, is currently being explored, but early results indicate a huge oil field, possibly the largest discovered in the past 30 years. A significant part of that oil is expected to reach customers in the West via new pipelines. One recently completed pipeline—the Caspian Pipeline Consortium or CPC—carries oil from the Tengiz field to the Russian Black Sea port of Novorossisk, where it is loaded onto sea-going tankers. After years of negotiations and planning, in September 2002 construction began on a new 1,090-mile (1,754-km) pipeline that will run from the western Caspian Sea coast through Azerbaijan, Georgia, and Turkey to the Turkish port of Ceyhan on the Mediterranean coast. Called the Baku-Tbilisi-Ceyhan (BTC) pipeline, it is attractive to Kazakhstan because it will bypass Russia and thereby loosen Moscow's grip on the Kazakh economy. The pipeline also is supported by the United States, mainly because it also bypasses Iran, a country hostile to the United States. It is expected to cost $2.9 billion and be completed in 2008.

CLIMATE

Kazakhstan may be rich in oil, but it is poor in an even more important liquid: water. Its precarious water situation is illustrated each year when many of its rivers and lakes evaporate in the baking summer heat. The country's climate is strongly continental, with hot summers and cold winters. Rainfall is light, most of the country receiving between four and eight inches (10–20 cm) of rain per year. South-central desert regions receive even less. Summer rainfall on the steppe grasslands often comes in the form of heavy summer thunderstorms that can cause flash flooding. Precipitation in the eastern mountain regions, usually in the form of snow, is significantly higher, averaging the equivalent of more than 23 inches (60 cm) of rain per year. In a few areas in the Altai Mountains, precipitation can top 59 inches (150 cm) per year.

SATANIC MILLS AND ATOMIC ILLS

When the Soviet Union collapsed in 1991, it left a poisonous residue of environmental pollution and ecological damage across the width and breadth of Eurasia, from the Baltic to the Pacific coast and from the Arctic Circle to the shores of the Black and Caspian Seas and the deserts of Central Asia. Some of the worst and longest-lasting damage was in Kazakhstan. The destruction of the Aral Sea was only one of the environmental disasters that Kazakhstan inherited from the Soviet era.

Some of the most visible damage came from enormous metallurgical factories that processed Kazakhstan's large deposits of lead, zinc, copper, and iron. One example was a lead smelter in the southern city of Chimkent, where 5,000 employees worked amid poisonous lead fumes that damage the body's nervous system. They were protected by nothing but thin cotton masks. In the eastern city of Oskemen (Ust-Kamenogorsk during the Soviet era) near the Russian border, trees lining wide boulevards survived despite the pollution from factories producing nickel, zinc, lead, uranium, and other metals. These factories made Oskemen one of the most polluted cities in Kazakhstan. Three large factories producing phosphorous compounds in the southern city of Dzhambul filled the air with smoke containing compounds that were both carcinogenic and corrosive to the lungs. No wonder the Western journalist who photographed these and other factories in 1992 referred to them as "Kazakhstan's Dark Satanic Mills." Two years later, another Western journalist, visiting a plant in Oskemen that processed uranium into fuel rods for nuclear power plants, reported that "the plant's tailings set my radiation meter buzzing as I stood 300 yards away." He added that Kazakh investigators had found lead and zinc "in the soil, in the cucumbers of home gardens, in water, in air, in mother's milk." It therefore was no surprise that medical examinations found 58 percent of the local children had immune-system abnormalities, or that of 103 young people tested, 60 had chromosome damage. Indeed, an earlier investigation during the Soviet era that was suppressed by the authorities found, in the journalist's words, that the "entire population was laced with lead."

Industrial pollution was only the beginning of the dreadful story. On August 29, 1949, the northeastern Kazakh steppe between the cities of Semey (Soviet-era name: Semipalatinsk) and Pavlodar literally shook, and a huge fireball lit up the sky. The Soviet Union had tested its first atomic bomb. A scientist about 10 miles from ground zero described what he witnessed:

On top of the tower an unbearably bright light blazed up. For a moment or two it dimmed and then with new force began to grow quickly. The white fireball engulfed the tower and the shop and, expanding rapidly, changing color, it rushed upwards. The blast wave at the base, sweeping in its path structures, stone houses, machines, rolled like a billow from the center, mixing up stones, logs of wood, pieces of metal, and dust into one chaotic mass. The fireball, rising and revolving, turned orange, red. Then dark streaks appeared. Streams of dust, fragments of brick and board were drawn in after it, as into a funnel. Overtaking the firestorm, the shock wave, hitting the upper layers of the atmosphere, passed through several levels of inversion, and there, as in a cloud chamber, the condensation of water vapor began.

. . . A strong wind muddled the sound, and it reached us like a roar of an avalanche. Above the testing ground there grew a grey column of sand, dust, and fog with a copula-shaped top, intersected by two tiers of cloud and layers of inversion. The upper part . . . reaching a height of 6–8 kilometers, recalled a copula of cumulus storm-clouds. The atomic mushroom was blown to the south, losing its outlines, and turning into a formless torn heap of clouds one might see after a gigantic fire.

The August 1949 explosion was the first of 456 nuclear tests, 116 in the atmosphere and the rest underground, that the Soviet regime conducted at its Semipalatinsk nuclear test site in Kazakhstan. It was, by far, the Soviet Union's busiest test site. With the development of thermonuclear, or hydrogen, bombs—bombs based on the principle of fusion rather than fission—in the 1950s, many of the explosions dwarfed the one test of August 1949. Some of them cracked walls in towns more than 50 miles from the test site. The Soviet Union's first fusion-type device, 20 times more powerful than the August 1949 bomb, was tested at Semipalatinsk in August 1953. Its first true hydrogen fusion bomb, whose explosive force of 1.6 million tons of TNT made it more than 70 times more powerful than the August 1949 test, was detonated in the Kazakh sky in November 1955. After the Soviet Union signed the 1963 treaty that banned nuclear tests in the atmosphere, all tests were conducted underground. Altogether, the hundreds of atomic tests the Soviet Union conducted in Kazakhstan were equal to about 20,000 of the bombs they

The last Soviet nuclear test in Kazakhstan took place in 1989, and the Semipalatinsk nuclear test site was closed shortly thereafter. But the facility itself was not fully destroyed until this explosion sealed its last remaining tunnel on July 29, 2000. (AP/Wide World Photos/ Michael Rothbart)

exploded on August 29, 1949, a bomb about the same size as the one that destroyed the city of Hiroshima in 1945.

The actual test area, known as the Polygon, covered an area of 7,000 square miles (18,000 sq km), but winds spread fallout that contaminated an area of more than 116,000 square miles (300,000 sq km). People living in that region often were not warned about the tests or, if necessary, evacuated. In 1992, the Kazakh government estimated that 1.6 million people were exposed to radiation during those tests. Kazakhstan's top ecology official observed angrily, "The people were rabbits for experiments." The impact on their health has been devastating. Between 1960 and 1988 the percentage of stillbirths doubled. Rates of neurological disorders, anemia, and retardation increased drastically, as did cancers such as leukemia. The Soviet government tried to cover up what was happening, blaming rising cancer rates and other illnesses on other causes. They even suggested that one cause of rising cancers was the Kazakh habit of drinking extremely hot tea.

One of the most visible reminders of the invisible poisons from the Soviet atomic tests is Lake Balapan, also known as Atomic Lake. It is a crater about 1,640 feet (500 m) in diameter and 290 feet (100 m) deep caused by an underground atomic test in 1965. The goal of what the Soviets called a "peaceful" test was to create a reservoir, and waters from a nearby river were later diverted to fill the crater. In order to create the crater, the test was carried out near the surface, with the result that radiation escaped into the atmosphere and exposed people downwind. Today radiation levels in and near the lake remain dangerously high.

Nuclear testing in Kazakhstan finally stopped in 1989, in part because of local protests, which became possible during the era of perestroika under Mikhail Gorbachev. After the unsuccessful August 1991 coup against Gorbachev, Kazakh president Nazarbayev finally closed down the Polygon test site permanently. Tens of thousands of former Soviet soldiers and scientists then left the region, dealing a severe blow to the region's economy.

Nuclear tests are not the only source of dangerous radiation in Kazakhstan. Uranium mining and processing has left hundreds of millions of tons of low-level and medium-level waste in four locations. In 2000, a United Nations report concluded that those wastes represent "an especially serious problem in Kazakhstan." No country in the world has suffered worse from the aftereffects of nuclear fallout and radiation from industries related to making nuclear weapons than Kazakhstan.

Nuclear testing and the general problem of pollution were closely related to another activity, the Soviet space program, one of the great successes of the Soviet regime. The most important Soviet spacecraft launching site was the Baikonur Cosmodrome in southern Kazakhstan. It has been the launching site for every manned Soviet and (since 1992) Russian spaceflight since Yuri Gagarin became the first human to rocket into space and orbit the earth in 1961. The space and missile programs brought economic development to the area around Baikonur, but they also left toxic residues from spent rocket fuel and other wastes from empty fuel tanks that never reached orbit and crashed back to earth. After the collapse of the Soviet Union, Russia continued to rent Baikonur from Kazakhstan for $115 million per year, a fee that included keeping the base under complete Russian control. In mid-2002, Russia announced that all military satellites henceforth would be launched from a Russian site, a decision that reduced the activity at Baikonur.

The People of Kazakhstan:
A Changing Patchwork

As of mid-2001, Kazakhstan had a population of 16.7 million, divided into more than 100 different national and ethnic groups, almost all of them very small. At independence, Kazakhs were a plurality of 40 percent of the population, barely more than the Russian share of 38 percent. This changed dramatically within a decade. By 2001, as a result of a high ethnic Kazakh birthrate and the emigration of many ethnic Russians and other Europeans, the Kazakhs were a majority, accounting for more than 53 percent of the total population. Russians, still by far the largest minority, were about 30 percent of the population. Ukrainians accounted for 3.7 percent, Uzbeks for 2.5 percent, and ethnic Germans for 2.4 percent. About 47 percent of the total population was Muslim and about 44 percent Russian Orthodox. Between 1992 and 1997, more than 1.6 million people, mainly Russians, Ukrainians, and ethnic Germans, emigrated from Kazakhstan. The pace of emigration, which had been slowing between 1994 and 1997, then picked up again. By the end of the decade, the country's ethnic German population had declined by two-thirds and the Ukrainian population by a third. This emigration may have pleased Kazakh nationalists determined to increase their share of the total population, but it cost the country a significant part of its best educated and technically skilled workforce. President Nazarbayev, for example, expected and wanted to see a more gradual change in the country's Kazakh-Russian demographic balance. The government meanwhile encouraged Kazakhs to have large families and tried to attract some of the approximately 4.1 million Kazakhs living abroad—including 1.5 million in Uzbekistan, 740,000 in Russia, 700,000 in Turkmenistan, and 1.5 million in China—to immigrate to their newly independent homeland. The effort succeeded in attracting only 170,000 people, a total that may have been matched by the number of ethnic Kazakhs who emigrated from Kazakhstan during that period. Still, the process of what has been called "Kazakhification" meant that Kazakhstan's population increasingly would be more Kazakh, less European, and less diverse.

One of Kazakhstan's most positive statistics when it became independent was its high literacy rate. A legacy of the Soviet educational system, literacy stood at 98 percent: 99 percent for men and 96 percent for women. Those impressive figures declined in the following decade, although by how much is uncertain. What is clear is that budget cuts and a variety of other factors, including the revival of traditional Muslim attitudes, kept children from attending school. Compounding the problem, fewer qualified teachers were available because during the 1990s many left their poorly paid profession for better-paying jobs. Official statistics indicate that school attendance fell only slightly during the first half of the 1990s. However, unofficial sources indicate that by 1997, 20 percent of Kazakhstan's school-age population, mainly girls, was at home rather than in school.

CULTURE AND DAILY LIFE

The Kazakhs were nomads for most of their history. That has changed since the Russian conquest of the region, and today, while a majority of Kazakhs still live in rural areas, most are settled in towns or villages. Still, nomadic traditions persist in many areas of Kazakh life, from literature and music to food and sports.

The nomadic Kazakhs did not have a written language. Until the mid-19th century, their literature consisted primarily of long oral poems. These epic poems were recited by elders called *akyns*, who often chanted their sagas accompanied by traditional hand-held drums and a small two-stringed musical instrument similar to a lute called a *dombra*. The most common themes were the heroic deeds of Kazakh warriors. Several of the most important poems that have survived involve warfare against the Kalmyks, nomads who came from Mongolia and threatened the Kazakhs for generations. One of the most revered *akyns*, Zhambyl Zhambayev (1846–1945), had a town in southern Kazakhstan named after him. *Akyn* performances still are very popular in Kazakhstan, as are traditional contests between *akyns*, which are known as *aitys*. Among the country's amateur performers is none other than President Nazarbayev, who has sung and played the *dombra* on television.

Written Kazakh literature dates from the work of the 19th-century writer, poet, and translator Abay Ibrahim Kunanbayev (1845–1904). Aside from writing many stories and poems, which he recited in public readings, Kunanbayev translated Russian and other foreign literature into

Kazakh. One of the foreign stories he translated and read that was picked up by other poets and became very popular among the Kazakhs was *The Three Musketeers*, by French writer Alexander Dumas. Today there are two museums honoring Kunanbayev's memory, one in the city of Semey, where he spent much of his life, and the other in the small village of Zhidebai, where the man considered the father of modern Kazakh literature died.

The Kazakh diet is another legacy of a nomadic past. Central Asian nomads traditionally ate large amounts of meat from sheep and horses, and the Kazakhs still do that today. The national dish, *besbarmak*, consists of boiled meat—either beef, mutton, or horsemeat—served atop a base of noodles, potatoes, and onions. Its name means "five fingers," which describes how it traditionally was eaten. The guest of honor in a Kazakh home often will be given a sheep's head that has been cooked in a special way. Kazakhs eat a variety of dishes made from horsemeat, including a sausage-like dish wrapped in horse intestines. They also enjoy dishes popular throughout Central Asia, including *plov*, an Uzbek rice dish that Kazakhs make with dried apricots, raisins, prunes, and other ingredients. In the cities, the past two centuries of Kazakhstan's history is reflected by the popularity of Russian cuisine.

Kazakhs who eat traditional foods in restaurants often find themselves in settings made to look like yurts, the tent-like traditional nomad dwelling. The yurt is a portable structure consisting of a flexible wood frame covered by an inner layer of woven mats and an outer layer of felt coated with sheep fat for waterproofing. Designed to be assembled or dismantled in less than an hour, the yurt was remarkably snug in winter and cool in summer. Yurt floors and walls were decorated by colorful felt and wool carpets made by hand. Today fewer and fewer yurts dot the steppe, but they are set up in towns as part of holiday celebrations. In addition, the yurt design often serves as a decorative motif in public buildings.

The Kazakhs, like other nomads of inner Asia, were skilled horsemen. Those skills are still very much in evidence at traditional festivals, where a variety of contests take place on horseback. One popular event is a grueling race in which young boys ride bareback for 30 laps around a mile-long track. Another is a chase in which a young boy attempts to catch a girl; as his horse gets close to hers, she fends him off with a whip. The boy's reward if he succeeds before the girl reaches the finish line is a kiss.

Yet another match between mounted contestants involves two young men who wrestle and try to throw one another to the ground. That event is a test of both physical strength and extraordinary horsemanship.

Daily life in Kazakhstan is in many ways shaped by the country's painful economic problems. According to a United Nations report, in 2000 about 65 percent of the population lived in poverty. A study done in 1999 found that one-third of the people could not feed their families satisfactorily, a number that rose to more than 63 percent in western Kazakhstan, the poorest part of the country. Health care deteriorated during the 1990s as spending fell far below Soviet-era levels. The incidence of infectious diseases such as tuberculosis soared, as did AIDS, which spread as drug use increased among the population, especially young people. While statistics varied, a reasonable guess was that life expectancy during the first half of the 1990s fell by two to four years.

Violent crime and criminality also have a large impact on daily life. Organized crime is widespread, in part because of Central Asia's growing narcotics trade. Corporate executives travel to and from work with armed bodyguards. Criminal gangs, aside from running illegal drug, weapons, and prostitution rings, prey on legitimate businesses. Violence, including murder, is a common way of influencing business deals. Overall, the rule of law has not yet been established in Kazakhstan; the people know this and therefore do not expect that legal authorities will be able to protect them.

Another important factor in daily life is the growing influence of Islam. Between 1989 and 1996, the number of Islamic institutions increased from fewer than 50 to more than 600, and that figure had doubled by 2002. Islamic influence was most pronounced in southern Kazakhstan, the home of most of the country's Uzbek minority. At the same time, young people between 18 and 29 constituted the largest group of believers among the Kazakh population, an important sign for future trends. The government meanwhile increased its efforts to repress Islamic extremists, a campaign that included arresting militant missionaries from countries such as Pakistan, Egypt, and Sudan. As one expert has observed, "Kazakhstan is the only Central Asian state that can truly call itself secular since it is the only state in the region that has not accorded Islam a special role." The people who govern the country and their supporters clearly intend to keep it that way.

Politics and Government

On December 16, 1991, the Kazakhstan Soviet Socialist Republic became the independent Republic of Kazakhstan. Just before that date, as the Soviet Union fell apart, two developments set the tone of political life in the new Republic of Kazakhstan. First, in September, President Nursultan Nazarbayev resigned his leadership posts in the Soviet Union's Communist Party and ordered its branch in Kazakhstan to be dissolved. Even though many of its top leaders, minus Nazarbayev, reorganized as the Socialist Party of Kazakhstan (SPK), the old Soviet one-party dictatorship was dead in Kazakhstan. Second, barely two months later, on December 1, 1991, 15 days before Kazakhstan declared its independence, Nazarbayev, running unopposed, was reelected president with 98.8 percent of the vote. To be fair, Nazarbayev was a very popular local leader, and it is hard to imagine that any other local politician could have defeated him in a fair multi-candidate election. But that type of presidential election did not take place, not in December 1991 nor in the decade that followed. Nazarbayev and his supporters, schooled in the Soviet system of one-party dictatorial government, had one paramount political goal: to build a strong Kazakh state. They were interested in political stability and a strong government that could introduce policies and reforms that would promote economic growth. They had no familiarity with democracy and, in any event, did not believe in it. Aside from viewing democracy as a threat to their power, they saw it as an obstacle to their ability to govern effectively. They believed that while communism certainly was finished, only an authoritarian form of government could ensure their country's future. Despite some opposition, Nazarbayev built that type of government in Kazakhstan during its first 10 years of independence.

TWO NEW CONSTITUTIONS AND PRESIDENTIAL POWER

When Kazakhstan was part of the Soviet Union, Communist Party leaders, including Nazarbayev, were able to rule Kazakhstan without facing organized opposition. One of the first things that Nazarbayev found out as president of an independent Kazakhstan was that this was no longer possible. Not being a member of the SPK, he was unable to control that political party. Of greater concern was the newly organized Congress Party (People's Congress of Kazakhstan, or NKK), headed by two prominent poets, Mukhtar Shakhanov and Olzhas Suleimenov. It stressed an anti-nuclear program and opposition to Nazarbayev's authoritarian tendencies and, in Suleimenov, produced a potential serious rival to the president. In June 1992, more than 5,000 people demonstrated in Almaty against Nazarbayev's government. The legislature demanded the resignations of the president's chosen prime minister and cabinet. Other groups, with varying agendas—from Kazakh nationalism to protecting the interests of ethnic Russian citizens—further complicated Nazarbayev's efforts to dominate Kazakh political life. A new constitution, introduced in January 1993, increased presidential powers and also marked an important symbolic break with the Soviet era. It did not, however, give Nazarbayev as much power as he later decided he wanted.

Kazakhstan's president did increase his international prestige during his first two years in office, especially by skillfully handling a tense situation involving nuclear weapons. Prior to 1991, the Soviet government had placed a large number of nuclear missiles in Kazakhstan. When the Soviet Union collapsed, those missiles were still there, in effect making Kazakhstan the world's fourth-largest nuclear power. Kazakhstan—along with Ukraine and Belarus, both of which became nuclear powers in the same way—immediately came under heavy international pressure to give up the weapons, a drive led by the United States. Kazakhstan quickly agreed to give up its weapons, which it was in no position to operate, maintain, or even protect. It signed two treaties—the Strategic Arms Reduction Treaty (START) in 1992, and the Treaty on Non-Proliferation of Nuclear Weapons (NPT) in 1993—under which it gave up its nuclear weapons and pledged not to acquire any in the future. American payments of about $1.5 billion, mainly for enriched uranium in the missile warheads, were an important incentive for the Kazakh government to conclude the negotiations. In 1994, a quickly organized airlift removed half a ton of weapons-grade uranium from a poorly protected Kazakh storage facility and brought it to the United States. By May 1995, Kazakhstan was free of all nuclear weapons.

Local political developments were less positive, particularly from the point of view of those who supported democracy. Kazakhstan's first post-

Soviet parliamentary elections, held in March 1994, were marred by irregularities. Many potential candidates, primarily ethnic Russians and opponents of Nazarbayev, were disqualified and kept off the ballot. When the votes were counted, to no one's surprise, an assortment of groups supporting the president won a plurality in the new one-chamber assembly, the Supreme Kenges. Still, Nazarbayev often found himself struggling to control the legislature when several parties got together to form an opposition bloc. That group included a newly revived Communist Party of Kazakhstan (KPK), which was allowed to legally reestablish itself in March of 1994. This was also the period local journalists operated relatively freely, an era that proved to be short-lived in the face of government pressures against the media that began during the second half of the 1990s.

In 1995, Kazakhstan went through a political crisis that strengthened Nazarbayev's power. In February, the country's top court declared the 1994 elections null and void because of voting irregularities, which in some districts had resulted in more votes being counted than the actual number of voters. After first appearing to be on the defensive, Nazarbayev, using emergency powers granted him in 1990, arranged a referendum on extending his presidential term to December 2000. More than 91 percent of Kazakhstan's voters dutifully went to the polls and, again to no one's surprise, 95.8 percent of them approved the extension. A few months later, voters were asked to approve a new constitution that significantly strengthened presidential powers. The government claimed that voter turnout topped 90 percent and that 89 percent voted for the constitution; opposition parties, which boycotted the referendum, claimed that less than half the voters went to the polls. In any event, Kazakhstan ended up with a new constitution and a government dominated by the president. The president was head of state, commander-in-chief of the armed forces, and empowered to appoint the cabinet and dissolve the legislature. In the new bicameral (two chamber) legislature, the president appointed seven of the 47-member upper chamber, or Senate, the rest being elected by various regional bodies. The lower chamber, the 67-member Majlis, was elected directly by the voters. The year 1995 ended with elections marred by irregularities that left parties supporting President Nazarbayev in control of both houses.

A PATTERN OF REPRESSION

More of the same followed during the next five years. Constitutional amendments in 1998 lengthened the presidential term to seven years and removed the previous two-term limit on holding that office. In 1998, a decision was made to hold presidential elections in 1999 rather than in 2000. Simultaneously, several opposition figures were declared ineligible to run for the presidency based on a variety of trumped-up offenses. Nazarbayev then was reelected with more than 80 percent of the vote in January 1999 after a campaign that international bodies heavily criticized for serious violations of fair election standards, among them the exclusion of key opposition candidates. Elections to the Senate and Majlis later in the year were subject to similar criticisms.

Harassment of Nazarbayev's political opponents continued into the new century. The best known was Akezhan Kazhegeldin, who served as prime minister from 1994 to 1997 before running afoul of Nazarbayev, mainly because he was a potential rival to the president. In 1999, Kazhegeldin was charged with a series of offenses including tax evasion and eventually left Kazakhstan for exile in Europe. That turned out to be a wise decision, as in September 2001 the former prime min-

President Nursultan Nazarbayev, pictured here in Kazakhstan's new capital of Astana in 1998, has become increasingly authoritarian and corrupt since leading his country to independence in 1991. (AP/Wide World Photos/Mikhail Metzel)

ister was tried in absentia for corruption and sentenced to 10 years at hard labor. In September 2000, an opposition figure named Lira Bayseitova was beaten up so severely that she nearly died. In 2002, two other leading opponents of Nazarbayev, Galymzhan Zhakiyanov and Mukhtar Ablyazov, cofounders in late 2001 of a pro-democracy group called Democratic Choice for Kazakhstan, were arrested and convicted of corruption while serving as government officials. Zhakiyanov, a former provincial governor who had a heart condition and was in failing health, was sentenced to seven years in prison. Ablyazov, formerly a government minister for energy, industry, and trade, received a six-year sentence. The U.S. State Department issued a statement saying the convictions appeared to be part of an effort to intimidate political opponents of the Nazarbayev regime.

A PATTERN OF CORRUPTION

The use of corruption charges to imprison or threaten political opponents was ironic at best. Nazarbayev's government was corrupt from top to bottom. Those profiting from their closeness to the president included members of his family, many of whom held important government or business positions. It also included people like Kazhegeldin, who enriched himself and his associates before his falling out with Nazarbayev. By the end of the decade, Nazarbayev, members of his family, and other close associates had made uncounted millions, and possibly billions, taking bribes from foreign investors and in a variety of deals involving the country's burgeoning oil industry. Their newly acquired wealth made possible incidents such as a $250,00 shopping spree during a presidential visit to a foreign country in 1996. The Nazarbayev family's influence, and its ability to profit from it, extended to every part of the country's economy. One notorious scandal was a secret national oil fund, into which Nazarbayev had diverted more than $1 billion by 2002. While government officials claimed that the money was intended to help the Kazakh economy out of a crisis that began in 1998, the secrecy surrounding it supported claims that the money was headed for the pockets of the Nazarbayev family. In fact, one of the main reasons that Zhakiyanov and Ablyazov had gotten into political trouble is that they had called for an investigation into Nazarbayev's foreign bank accounts. Although they could do nothing

THE PRESS UNDER SIEGE

The trend toward political dictatorship in Kazakhstan has taken its toll on the press. During the early 1990s, a relatively free press, both in print journalism and broadcasting, was developing.

What appeared to be a promising situation changed for the worse beginning in 1995 when Nazarbayev moved against his political opponents. The government drastically raised fees radio and television stations had to pay for licenses, forcing more than 30 of them to close. The license for the one independent television station ended up in the hands of Nazarbayev's eldest daughter, Dariga. The publisher of the country's largest and most popular independent newspaper was pressured to retire from journalism, and his business soon ended up in the hands of the Nazarbayev family. The publication that replaced it as Kazakhstan's major opposition newspaper had its offices firebombed in 1998, after which it suspended publication. In just one year, 1998, a new press law subjected other independent media outlets to more than 200 criminal investigations.

If the struggle for a free press in Kazakhstan has a poster child, it is Irina Petrushova, a 36-year-old ethnic Russian and founder and publisher of the weekly newspaper *Respublika.* Born in Russia, Petrushova came with her family to Kazakhstan during the Soviet era when her father, a journalist working for the Communist Party newspaper *Pravda,* was assigned to cover Kazakhstan. She married in 1984, attended college in Russia, and became a mother. After returning to Kazakhstan with her husband, she followed her father into journalism by taking over a struggling weekly financial newspaper. That paper eventually became the *Respublika,* which Petrushova founded in 2000.

Petrushova understood she had not chosen an easy path. Her father, Albert Petrushov, although a Communist, had been independent-minded and even during the Soviet era had exposed corruption in high places. Ironically, nothing happened to him prior to the collapse of the Soviet Union, but in 1992, Kazakhstan's first year of independence, he was run down by a car. Few people believed the incident was an accident. The brain injuries Petrushov suffered left him an invalid. His just-completed manuscript on corruption in Kazakhstan during the 1980s was stolen as he lay unconscious after the accident.

Her father's fate did not deter Irina, who soon turned the *Respublika* into a vehicle for exposing corruption and promoting human rights.

The government's response was not long in coming. Late in 2001, it tried to buy a controlling share in the paper. When that tactic failed, threats began. Four printers in succession stopped working with the newspaper, one after he found a human skull on his doorstep. In February 2002, the government charged Petrushova with criminal business violations that eventually resulted in a suspended jail sentence. In March, on International Women's Day, an important holiday during the Soviet era, Petrushova received a funeral wreath from an anonymous sender. A few days later, a court suspended the *Respublika* from publishing for three months. Petrushova responded by publishing her newspaper under several other easily recognizable names such as *Respublika on Fire* and *All that Respublika*. The anonymous threats then became more graphic, and more menacing. In May 2002 a decapitated dog appeared outside the newspaper with a note reading "There will be no next time." The next day the dog's head appeared outside Petrushova's apartment door with yet another note, this one saying "There will be no last time." Then the newspaper's offices were firebombed. Yet Petrushova remained undeterred. When the government began proceedings to take away the license for *Respublika,* she got another license for a new newspaper, the *Republic Business Review.*

Petrushova was not Kazakhstan's only journalist, and hers was not its only news outlet, under attack. In March 2002, an independent television station tried to cover an opposition rally called to protest the arrests of Mukhtar Abliyazov and Ghalymzhan Zhakiyanov. The rally was scheduled for March 29. But on March 28, gunmen attacked the station, destroying its broadcasting equipment in a hail of gunfire. Another newspaper had two of its journalists attacked and its equipment destroyed, while a publishing house was the victim of an arson attack. In August 2002, a prominent journalist, Sergei Duvanov, was beaten right outside his apartment in Almaty after reporting on Nazarbayev's corruption. According to the International League for Human Rights (ILHR), the attackers, who used rubber truncheons, warned, "You know what this is for. Next time, we'll leave you paralyzed." Worst of all, in mid-2002, the daughter of an opposition publisher was murdered. There were other incidents as well. One reporter for the *Republic Business Review* told an international group called the Institute for War and Peace Reporting that "This is what happens when you start criticizing the president, his family members, or his policy." As for Petrushova, who has hired an armed guard to protect her two sons, she asked an American reporter, "We're journalists. If not us, then who?"

about it, the people of Kazakhstan understood what was going on. In a poll taken in 2000, more than 43 percent of all respondents listed corruption as their country's most serious problem.

The Economy

Before 1991, Kazakhstan had been a major supplier of raw materials, agricultural products—especially wheat—and manufactured goods to the other parts of the Soviet Union. Most of its manufacturing was concentrated in industries such as metallurgy, petrochemicals, machine tools, food processing, and textiles. As elsewhere, after independence living standards in Kazakhstan deteriorated, as both industry and agriculture went through hard times. A large percentage of the 1993 wheat harvest was lost because of inefficient harvesting and poor transport and storage facilities, all legacies of the Soviet era. Local industries, including 50 large factories that at one time accounted for more than 11 percent of Soviet military production, suffered when demand from Russia and other parts of the Soviet Union collapsed.

The largest annual decline occurred in 1994, when industrial production fell by 25 percent. By the end of 1995, Kazakhstan's economy was less than half the size it had been in 1991. The economy finally grew during 1996–97, but went into another period of decline and recession in 1998. That reversal was caused by a financial crisis in Russia, still Kazakhstan's most important trading partner, and a fall in world oil prices, which lowered the value of Kazakhstan's exports. Rising international oil prices beginning in 1999 and a good grain harvest brought a return to economic growth that continued through 2000 and 2001 into 2002. During 2001, the economy grew by more than 13 percent, mainly as a result of foreign investment in the country's oil and natural gas industries. By 2001, foreign companies had invested more than $13 billion in those industries, and the oil industry alone accounted for almost a third of the government's total revenue. Still, in 2001, per capita income—the amount earned per person—was barely half of what it had been a decade earlier.

While the Kazakh economy was being shaken by the breakup of the Soviet Union and exposure to international markets, it also was going through the difficult process of privatization. In the first stage of privatization, state-owned apartments became the property of their occupants. Small stores and similar businesses also were privatized during this first stage. The second stage of privatization began in 1993 and involved medium-size businesses and factories. Each citizen received what was called a voucher, a document with a specified value that could be invested as its owner saw fit. The main beneficiaries of this process were people with connections to government leaders or a few shrewd operators, and a small number of people ended up with control of the most valuable businesses, while ordinary citizens ended up with little or nothing. The next stage of privatization focused on the largest and most valuable factories in the country. These were privatized in auctions that once again enriched the well connected, especially those closest to President Nazarbayev. One source of their wealth was under-the-table payments from foreign investors, who bought troubled but potentially valuable properties at very low prices.

The overall privatization process went unevenly. By the late 1990s, most small businesses were in private hands, but only about 11 percent of medium-size enterprises and less than 5 percent of Kazakhstan's largest enterprises. Privatization had the least effect on agriculture. Officially, Soviet-era collective farms were privatized, with members turned into shareholders. In reality, they remained intact, operating as inefficiently as ever. Agricultural land remained unprivatized. While individuals and corporations could purchase the right to use land, and sell that right to others, ownership remained with the state.

Foreign investment was vital to privatizing and modernizing Kazakhstan's largest enterprises. The majority of that investment went into the oil and natural gas industries, where foreign skills and capital were essential to developing the country's oil and gas fields. Kazakhstan's iron, steel, and nonferrous metals industries also attracted foreign investors. One of the more interesting successful examples of investment in those industries involved the huge Karmat steel mill in the north-central Kazakh city of Temirtau. Karmat was the 67th-largest steel mill in the world in the mid-1990s. While working at only half its capacity, it produced 10 percent of Kazakhstan's gross domestic product (GDP). The giant plant, with seven coke ovens and four blast furnaces, covered 50 square miles. By 1995, like many similar enterprises throughout the former Soviet Union, Karmat was bankrupt and on the verge of collapse.

That year it was sold to a steel company from India, Ispat International, at a bargain price. The deal, like others in Kazakhstan, reportedly benefited Nazarbayev, who had worked there in the 1960s. Still, it was not easy for the new owners to make money. Ispat International had to invest hundreds of millions of dollars to modernize the outdated plant. To secure a regular supply of coal, it bought nearby coal mines. When the local electric power company broke down 16 times in 1996, Ispat International bought it as well. It later took over Temirtau's water supply system, trolley line, and a local textile factory, the last to supply its workers with uniforms. When the local city government could not pay for health services and teachers' salaries, the company helped pay those expenses as well. Ispat International even started a television station in Temirtau.

Ispat International finally earned its first profit from Karmat in late 1999. Temirtau's overall economy, however, remained depressed. There was widespread alcoholism and drug abuse. Rows of deserted apartment houses testified to the thousands of former residents who had left the city in search of better lives elsewhere. The 27,000 people who had jobs at the steel mill understood they were better off than most of their neighbors. As one of them put it, "It's not as good as in the old days, but it's better than starving."

In sum, a decade of economic change has produced more losers than winners. A small, well-connected elite has accumulated great wealth and has used it to enjoy fancy foreign cars, lavish new homes, and expensive trips abroad. Despite economic growth that began in the late 1990s, most people have a lower standard of living than when Kazakhstan first became independent. The national unemployment rate in 2002 was at least 14 percent, and probably much higher. It soared to as high as 50 percent in decaying industrial cities far away from the oil fields. Kazakhstan's industrial base and natural resources gave it the potential to build a modern industrial economy and provide its people with a decent standard of living, but that potential was a long way from realization.

NOTES

p. 91 " 'Kazakhstan's possible hydrocarbon reserves . . .' " U.S. Government Energy Information Administration, "Kazakhstan Country Analysis Brief." July 2002.

Available on-line. URL: http://www.eia.doe.gov/emeu/cabs/kazak.html. Downloaded September 11, 2002, p. 2.

p. 93 "Kazakhstan's Dark Satanic Mills" Sabastião Salgado, "Kazakhstan's Dark Satanic Mills," *The New York Times Magazine*, February 2, 1992, p. 23.

p. 93 " 'the plant's tailings set my radiation meter buzzing . . .' " Mike Edwards, "Lethal Legacy," *National Geographic* 186, no. 2 (August 1994), p. 91.

p. 93 "entire population was laced with lead" Mike Edwards, "Lethal Legacy," p. 92.

p. 94 " 'On top of the tower . . .' " Quoted in David Halloway, *Stalin and the Bomb: The Soviet Union and Atomic Energy, 1939–1956* (New Haven, Conn. and London: Yale University Press, 1994), p. 217.

p. 95 " 'The people were rabbits for experiments' " Quoted in Mike Edwards, "A Broken Empire," *National Geographic* 183, no. 3 (March 1993), p. 36.

p. 96 "an especially serious problem in Kazakhstan" Dr. Claus Bennerberg, "Environmental Performance Review of Kazakhstan 1999/2000: Management of Radioactively Contaminated Territories," July 15, 2002. Available on-line. URL: http://rrzn-user.unihanover.de/zrs/radio08.htm. Downloaded September 9, 2002, p. 2.

p. 100 " 'Kazakhstan is the only Central Asian state that can . . .' " Martha Brill Olcott, *Kazakhstan: Unfulfilled Promise* (Washington, D.C.: Carnegie Endowment for International Peace, 2002), p. 209.

p. 107 " 'You know what this is for . . .' " Quoted in Sabry Bozai, "Attack Against Journalist in Kazakhstan Indicative of Political Crisis—Human Rights Advocates," September 4, 2002, EurasiaNet Human Rights. Available on-line. URL: http://www.eurasianet.org/departments/rights/articles/eav090402.shtml. Downloaded September 6, 2002, p. 1.

p. 107 " 'This is what happens when you . . .' " *Russia's Week* (The Jamestown Foundation, Washington, D.C.), May 30, 2002, p. 5.

p. 107 " 'We're journalists . . .' " Quoted in *The New York Times*, July 13, 2002, p. A4.

p. 110 " 'It's not as good as in the old days . . .' " Quoted in *The New York Times*, August 1, 2001, p. A4.

8

UZBEKISTAN

Since ancient times, the geographic, cultural, economic, and population center of Central Asia has been the area between the Amy Darya and Syr Darya Rivers. Today most of that territory lies within Uzbekistan, and it retains much of its historic importance. Uzbekistan is the most populous of the Central Asian countries, with 50 percent more people than Kazakhstan, its nearest competitor. Large Uzbek communities in three of the four other Central Asian countries means that Uzbeks have a strong presence throughout the region. Uzbeks are the largest minority in Tajikistan, where they account for almost a quarter of the population. In Kyrgyzstan, they account for 13.8 percent of the population, and in Turkmenistan, they make up more than 9 percent. Only in Kazakhstan, where their share of the population is only 2.5 percent, are Uzbeks a relatively insignificant group in terms of size. Uzbekistan, while smaller in area than both Kazakhstan and Turkmenistan, remains Central Asia's geographic core. It alone borders on every other Central Asian republic. It is the region's leading military power, the only country in the region that has a manufacturing sector with an important engineering component, and the only one that competes in any way with Russia in influencing regional affairs. In short, along with Kazakhstan, Uzbekistan is one of the two heavyweights in Central Asia. This gives events that occur there a significance that extends beyond its own borders to all of its neighbors in the region.

A Country Map

Uzbekistan covers a predominantly arid area of about 172,700 square miles (447,400 sq km), making it slightly larger than California. It looks roughly like a single-clawed lobster facing eastward. Much of that claw, the easternmost part of the country, is formed by the fertile Fergana Valley, the most densely populated part of both Uzbekistan and the whole of Central Asia. Uzbekistan is bordered to the north and west for 1,368 miles (2,203 km) by Kazakhstan. About 130 miles (209 km) of that long border crosses the Aral Sea along a northwest to southeast diagonal. To Uzbekistan's south, across a border 1,007 miles (1,621 km) long, is Turkmenistan. A small stretch of that border in the west crosses the northern edge of Lake Saryqamysh, a huge, salty, and polluted puddle in a desert depression created in the 1960s by drainage from land irrigated by water from the Amy Darya. At the opposite end of the country, Uzbekistan has a short southern border with Afghanistan. To the east, across a jagged and complicated border that twists, turns, and juts for more than 1,400 miles (2,260 km), are Tajikistan and Kyrgyzstan.

About 80 percent of Uzbekistan is desert or arid steppe, and most of that is desert. Only about 10 percent of the country is arable. The westernmost part of the country, the area west of the Aral Sea, is the Ustyurt Plateau, a desolate region of salt marshes and a few streams that expire in the desert. The center of Uzbekistan is covered by the barren Qizilqum desert, which stretches northward into Kazakhstan. The main break in the desert is the Amu Darya delta, where amid dying wetlands and disappearing lakes the remnants of the once-mighty river trickle into what is left of the Aral Sea. Most of the western half of Uzbekistan is a lowland less than 660 feet (200 meters) above sea level.

In the eastern half of Uzbekistan, the land rises gradually until it reaches mountains that in the south continue into Tajikistan and in the north into Kyrgyzstan. Although the highest mountains are in those two small countries, some of Uzbekistan's peaks tower more than 14,600 feet (4,500 meters) above sea level. The far western regions, where foothills gradually turn into mountains, have life-giving water from mountain rivers that rise either in Tajikistan, Kyrgyzstan, or Afghanistan. The river farthest south, the Amu Darya, does little for eastern Uzbekistan, forming the country's border with Afghanistan before flowing into Turkmenistan. It remains in Turkmenistan for hundreds of miles before entering western Uzbekistan far downstream along a route northward to the Aral Sea. The most important river in eastern Uzbekistan is the Zeravshan, which enters the country from Tajikistan. The Zeravshan provides water for two ancient oasis cities and cultural centers—Samarkand (population: 370,000) and, farther downstream, Bukhara (population 240,000)—before disappearing into desert sands north of the Amu Darya.

Samarkand, Uzbekistan's "golden city," is the country's second most important urban center, after Tashkent. The ancient city, the most famous of the oasis cities along the Silk Road, has been casting its spell over visitors for more than 2,000 years. Known as Marakanda in the days of Alexander the Great, the city apparently so bewitched the Greek conqueror that shortly after leaving it he pronounced himself a god. Destroyed by Genghis Khan, it was rebuilt and restored to glory by Tamerlane. Though it fell into decline after 1700, the city's legend remained intact, as a British poet and diplomat dramatically noted in 1913:

> We travel not for trafficking alone:
> By hotter winds our fiery hearts are fanned:
> For lust of knowing what should not be known
> We make the Golden Journey to Samarkand.

Samarkand's most magnificent monument, the Registan or "Place of Sand," was built after Tamerlane's death. The Registan's first building was a *madrasa,* or Islamic seminary, built by Ulugh Beg, Tamerlane's grandson, on the west side of an enormous public square. Two others followed on other sides of the square in the mid-17th century, their outer walls, like Ulugh Beg's, covered with ceramic tiles arranged in countless stunning mosaic designs. Today the former *madrasas* grace three sides of the square, the size of two football fields, described by one awed British diplomat as "the noblest public square in the world." Ironically, the Registan owes its current good state of repair to a massive restoration project undertaken by the anti-religious Soviet regime. That effort included rebuilding domes and minarets, restoring damaged tile work, and in some places removing more than six feet of earth and garbage that had accumulated during several centuries of neglect.

The Registan in Samarkand, pictured here during the Eid celebration in 1992, is the centerpiece of the city and probably the most magnificent architectural monument in Central Asia. (United Nations)

A notable characteristic of both Samarkand and Bukhara is that the majority of their populations are Tajiks. Both cities have been associated with Tajik history and culture since ancient times. In the 1930s, nationalist-minded Tajiks were distraught when the Soviet regime drew borders that placed Samarkand and Bukhara within the Uzbek SSR. Since the collapse of the Soviet Union, Samarkand and Bukhara have been stranded on the other side of an international border, a development that has turned what originally was an insult to the Tajik people into a painful injury to the country of Tajikistan.

In the far north, in Uzbekistan's section of the Fergana Valley, two large tributaries flowing from Kyrgyzstan, the Naryn and the Kara Darya, meet to form the Syr Darya. As it leaves the valley, the Syr Darya crosses into Tajikistan before turning north and cutting across a neck of Uzbek territory en route to Kazakhstan and, ultimately, the northern shores of the Aral Sea. The Fergana Valley, the "garden of Uzbekistan," is considered the country's heartland. About 90 percent of its population of 8 million is ethnic Uzbek. That predominance sometimes has spelled trouble for other ethnic groups, who since independence have been moving out of the valley. In 1989, Uzbek riots directed against a small group known as Meskhetian Turks left hundreds dead. Uzbek mobs in the eastern city of Andijan attacked the city's Jewish community that same year, while in 1990 non-Uzbek Turks were victims of attacks in two districts in the valley.

For centuries the Fergana Valley produced a great variety of fruits and vegetables, but during the Soviet era much of its fertile farmland was converted to cotton production, and at one point the valley produced a quarter of the Soviet cotton crop. Since independence, Uzbek farmers have returned some of those fields to food crops.

About 50 miles northeast of the point where the Syr Darya leaves Uzbekistan for the second and last time is Tashkent, the country's capital. The city stands on an oasis along the Chirchic River, a tributary of the Syr Darya. With a population of more than 2.1 million, Tashkent, which means "city of stone" in Turkic, was the fourth-largest city in the Soviet Union and today is by far the largest city in Central Asia.

Tashkent's history as a trading and cultural center is 2,000 years old, but much evidence of that history was lost in 1966 when the city was leveled by an earthquake. In rebuilding according to standard Soviet style, with dreary apartment blocks, wide avenues, and large stretches of parkland, Soviet planners also gave Tashkent a modern subway system, the only one in Central Asia. The subway, constructed between 1972 and 1977, was built with extensive rubber padding to make it as earthquake-proof as possible.

In the post-Soviet era, many of Uzbekistan's Russian citizens who stayed in the country sought security and familiarity in Tashkent, and today perhaps half of the city's residents are Russian-speaking. One of the city's museums honors Alisher Navoi, the 15th-century poet who is considered the father of the modern Uzbek language. Navoi, who also was a skilled painter and sculptor, used his wealth to found many schools, hospitals, and mosques. Languages other than Uzbek and Russian are heard in Tashkent as well. Since independence other non-Uzbek minorities followed the Russian example and gathered in Tashkent. Together Tashkent's many non-Uzbeks give the city a cosmopolitan flavor rare in Central Asia.

CLIMATE

Uzbekistan is an arid country with a continental climate. Most of the rain, averaging between four and eight inches per year (10 to 20 cm), falls in the winter and spring. Summers are long and hot with temperatures in July averaging about 90°F (32°C) and often reaching 104°F (40°C) during the day. Winters, while short, are often very cold, with temperatures dropping as low as –36°F (–38°C). The sun shines for more than 300 days each year. Uzbekistan's mountains on its eastern fringe provide pleasant relief from the desert's summer heat, but winters there are bitterly cold and snowy.

NATURAL RESOURCES

Uzbekistan has deposits of natural gas, oil, coal, gold, uranium, copper, silver, and a number of other valuable nonferrous metals such as lead, zinc, tungsten, and lithium. However, its deposits of natural gas and oil do not compare with the massive deposits of Turkmenistan and Kazakhstan. Uzbekistan has just enough oil to meet its own needs, a government goal that was achieved during the 1990s. The country has enough natural gas to become a significant exporter—it currently is the world's 10th largest producer—but that will require millions of dollars in foreign investment to build new pipelines and refineries. Uzbekistan is, however, the world's eighth-largest producer of gold. It produces about 70 tons of gold per year from 30 mines, including the Murantau mine in the Qizilqum Desert, the largest open-cast gold mine in the world. Metals are an increasingly important export, second only to cotton. Cotton remains by far the most important agricultural crop, accounting for 40 percent of the value of all agricultural production. Uzbekistan draws some benefits from natural resources elsewhere in the region. Fifteen percent of its electricity comes from hydroelectric power generated by power stations on mountain rivers in Kyrgyzstan and Tajikistan.

Water, the most vital resource of all for human life, is in critically short supply in Uzbekistan. There is water in the mountainous eastern fringe of the country, but other areas face a serious water crisis. About 90 percent of Uzbekistan's water is used to irrigate crops, mainly cotton and rice, both extremely thirsty plants, and other crops. The country's irrigation system, poorly built during the Soviet era and inefficiently managed,

In 2002 the government told cotton farmers like these, 125 miles southwest of Tashkent, that in the future they would be required to sell only half their crop to the government at fixed prices. Many doubt that this reform will be carried out. (AI Photo, Uzbekistan)

wastes huge amounts of water. Since independence, agricultural yields of important crops have been consistently below government targets and in some cases have decreased in the face of water shortages and general mismanagement. Rice production has been the worst hit, declining from more than 420,000 tons in 1999 to less than 68,000 tons in 2001. As one farmer in the hard-hit western part of the country reported in mid-2002, "We have not had enough water for three years. A considerable portion of land has been damaged by desertification; my fellow countrymen are in sore distress. No cotton, no rice, no wheat." Pollution makes matters worse. Much of the drinking water in Uzbekistan is contaminated from agricultural or industrial wastes. The long-term prospect is grim: One survey in the 1990s found that almost all underground freshwater supplies were polluted by these wastes.

People

As of mid-2001, more than 25 million people lived in Uzbekistan. Uzbeks made up about 80 percent of the population. Russians, at 5.5 percent of the population, constituted the largest minority, though about 60,000 of them leave the country each year. Tajiks and Kazakhs respectively made up 5 and 3 percent of the population. With current trends, the Tajiks soon will be the largest ethnic minority in Uzbekistan. The next largest group, a Turkic people, are the Karakalpaks, who make up about 2.5 percent of the population. Approximately 100 tiny ethnic groups make up the rest of the population.

Despite their small numbers, the Karakalpaks occupy a special place in Uzbekistan. Karakalpakstan, one of the 13 political units of the country, has a unique status. The Karakalpaks are the largest single ethnic group in that thinly populated region, which occupies the eastern third of the country. Karakalpakstan is the only political division in the country without an Uzbek majority. Moreover, it alone officially has the status of being a semi-autonomous republic within Uzbekistan. In reality, Karakalpakstan is under the same tight central control as the rest of the country. Along with Uzbekistan's territory west of the Aral Sea, it includes the delta of the Amu Darya south of the sea as well as territory further east. About a third of the region's 1.3 million people are ethnic

Karakalpaks, a figure that gives them a narrow plurality. There are almost as many Uzbeks and slightly fewer Kazakhs. The Karakalpaks speak a language closer to Kazakh than Uzbek. Prior to being forced onto Soviet collective farms in the 1930s, they were mainly a nomadic and fishing people. Karakalpakstan, including the Amu Darya delta, is the part of Uzbekistan most affected by the environmental damage associated with the drying up of the Aral Sea. It also is the region with the most severe water shortages. Its people suffer from a variety of diseases and serious medical problems related to environmental pollution, including a tuberculosis epidemic, an infant mortality rate that is one of the highest in the world, and an anemia rate among women of almost 80 percent. Thirty percent of the region's tuberculosis victims are children, many of whom cannot attend school because of their poor health.

Uzbekistan remains a rural country: 62 percent of its people live in the countryside and 38 percent in cities and large towns. The population is growing at more than 2 percent per year, a rate dangerously high in terms of the burden it puts on the country's limited resources and the government's efforts to promote economic development and reduce poverty. About 88 percent of Uzbekistan's people are Muslims, mainly Sunnis, while 9 percent are Russian Orthodox.

CULTURE AND DAILY LIFE

Old cultural traditions still influence daily life in Uzbekistan. Elderly people enjoy a high status, especially the elderly men, or "white beards," who continue to dominate local neighborhood councils. Family bonds and the authority of parents are strong. It remains common for parents to arrange marriages, often without much input from the son or daughter involved. Young couples still frequently begin their lives together living in the household of the groom's parents, and they are expected to have children within a year. At the same time, relations between the generations are changing. It is no longer unusual for young men and women to meet on their own and decide to get married. Still, they often defer to their parents by asking them to arrange the marriage.

The old ways of dressing still are visible in Uzbekistan. Most older men wear the traditional black skullcap decorated with elaborate white embroidery. The skullcap is worn more often than the other characteristic male Uzbek garment: the long, loose cloak that is closed with a bright-colored sash. Uzbek women customarily wear bright dresses that reach the knee; trousers made of the same material are worn underneath. However, seven decades of Soviet rule and a decade of post-Soviet independence have had their impact. Younger men and some younger women in the cities wear Western clothing, with men preferring a white shirt and a jacket. That up-to-date outfit sometimes is combined with the traditional skullcap. There is, however, another trend in parts of the Fergana Valley, where strict Islamic values are spreading. In those areas, growing numbers of women are pressured to wear veils and black garments called chadors, which cover the entire body except the face.

Uzbeks remain proud of their traditional food. The national dish is *plov*, rice mixed with meat, vegetables, and fruit. Uzbeks prepare *plov* in about 100 different versions. Another popular dish is *shaslik*, skewered hunks of meat and fat cooked on a charcoal grill. Hot green tea is said to help digest heavy meals that often are high in both fat and cholesterol. In the summer, Uzbeks eat a large variety of locally grown fruit, including melons and grapes that have been famous for their quality and taste for centuries. Round unleavened bread called nan also has long been an important part of the Uzbek diet.

While foreign sports like soccer are popular in Uzbekistan, an ancient form of wrestling called *kurash* in recent years had been gaining the status of Uzbekistan's national sport. It started to enjoy a revival in Uzbekistan in the early 1980s, and received another boost in the early 1990s when the Karimov regime, as part of its campaign to restore Uzbek national values, began promoting the sport. It has developed a following outside Uzbekistan. In 1999 Tashkent hosted the first world *kurash* championship, which drew contestants from 48 different countries.

Like other Central Asians, the Uzbeks enjoy listening to traveling bards chant stories and epic poems accompanied by musical instruments. In the past, this was the main way these stories were made available to an illiterate population. Virtually all Uzbeks are literate today, but they still enjoy listening to traveling bards at holiday festivals. The country's most popular holiday is *Navruz* (New Days), which is celebrated throughout Central Asia. The holiday is an Islamic adaptation of ancient pre-Islamic celebrations marking the beginning of spring. After being discouraged and even banned for a while during the Soviet era, it was revived in 1989 as a concession to local sentiments. Aside from performances by bards and minstrels, the two-day holiday features street fairs, traditional games, music and drama festivals, feasting on special foods, and socializing.

Politics and Government

Since independence, Uzbekistan has been dominated by Islam Karimov. A longtime Communist Party functionary who reinvented himself as an Uzbek nationalist during the Gorbachev era, Karimov consolidated his personal dictatorship as Uzbekistan's president in the first year after independence. By the end of the decade, Uzbekistan's system of government could reasonably be called a sultanistic regime. Karimov's dominance of the country was virtually absolute. His portrait stared down at people in schools, hotel lobbies, stores, and almost everywhere else. Merely insulting the president was a crime that could bring a five-year jail sentence.

Aside from building a personal dictatorship, Karimov worked to promote Uzbek nationalism in order to unify the country and to build a strong centralized state able to assert its control over the country's far-flung regions. As Karimov saw it, the main threat to his power, and to Uzbekistan's prospects of becoming a modern and cohesive country, was militant (or fundamentalist) Islam. Karimov and his supporters understood that Islam as a religion was an important part of Uzbek identity. The president, though hardly a believer, even made the traditional Muslim pilgrimage to Islam's holiest sites in the city of Mecca in Saudi Arabia. But the former Communists-turned-nationalists who ruled Uzbekistan also were determined to keep Islam under control and far from the reins of political power. They considered fundamentalist Islam a reactionary and oppressive force and feared it would return the country to the backwardness of the Middle Ages. Karimov therefore was relentless in mobilizing Uzbekistan's army and police to crush militant Islamic groups, the most formidable of which was the Islamic Movement of Uzbekistan (IMU). At the same time, Karimov was determined to eliminate all opposition to or criticism of his rule, whether it came from religious or secular sources and whether the alternative being presented was authoritarian or democratic.

BUILDING THE NEW STATE
WITH POLITICAL REPRESSION

Post-Soviet Uzbekistan's political system took shape between August 1991 and December 1992. On August 31, 1991, the day it declared independence, Uzbekistan's parliament renamed the country the Republic of Uzbekistan. At the same time, Uzbekistan's branch of the Communist Party broke its ties with the Communist Party of the Soviet Union. In November it shed its old Communist skin and emerged as the People's Democratic Party of Uzbekistan (PDPU). On December 29, 1991, Uzbekistan's citizens voted twice: once in a referendum on whether to become independent and a second time to select a new president. More than 98 percent of the voters endorsed independence. About 86 percent voted to reelect Karimov as president, a figure undoubtedly inflated by electoral fraud. Karimov's main opponent, who won 12 percent of the vote, was a poet and politician named Muhammad Solikh, the founder of the non-Communist movement Erk (Freedom), which had been established in 1990. The country's most important opposition group, Birlik (Unity), was prevented from fielding a candidate. The unfairness of the election was a sign of things to come.

Still, as 1992 began, Karimov's power was not yet absolute, and for a while both Erk and Birlik were able to function, as were two newly formed Islamic parties. These groups had little influence, however, as the PDPU under Karimov's leadership controlled the government, much as the Communist Party had done during the Soviet era. During the year, Karimov tightened his grip. In January, he destroyed the power base of one potential rival by eliminating the post of vice president. Birlik and Erk, the main secular opposition movements, as well as Muslim groups, were harassed and their leading members subjected to brutal physical attacks. Karimov used the example of Tajikistan, where in 1992 an Islamic uprising sparked a civil war, as justification for his repressive measures. One of the Karimov regime's most effective instruments of social control was its use of the *mahallahs*, powerful neighborhood associations that governed many aspects of everyday life in traditional Uzbek society. The regime turned them into organs of local government and created them where they did not exist, thereby extending its tentacles down to the street level in cities, towns, and villages throughout the country.

In December 1992, a new constitution was introduced. It declared Uzbekistan to be a secular and democratic republic in which freedom of expression and human rights were guaranteed. The falsity of those guarantees was illustrated almost immediately. The constitution gave the president enormous powers. On the day it was adopted, three leading Uzbek opposition leaders attending a human rights conference in Kyrgyzstan were seized by Uzbek security police and accused of sedition. In 1993, both Birlik and Erk were banned. Two of Birlik's leaders, fearing for their physical safety, fled the country. The press was brought under government control. At the end of the year, mass media outlets were ordered to re-register with the government; those that were independent were outlawed. Ultimately, all media outlets ended up in the hands of the state or close allies of President Karimov. In 1994, when elections for the new 250 member parliament took place, to nobody's surprise the PDPU took 193 of the 250 seats. Supporters of Karimov also took the remaining 57 seats. The government reported that 94 percent of eligible voters took part in the election, which by any reasonable democratic standards was without meaning. Voters went to the polls again in 1995. This time 99.3 percent of them supposedly cast their ballots to approve an extension of Karimov's presidential term, due to expire in 1997, to the year 2000. Another political event without meaning took place in 1996 when Karimov announced he was leaving the PDPU so, as Uzbekistan's head of state, he could guarantee its constitution in a non-partisan manner.

The only attempt to establish a democratic opposition group that had even temporary success occurred in 1995 with the formation of the Democratic Opposition Coordinating Center. It was led by Shakrulla Mirsaidov, the man who had been vice president when Karimov abolished that post in 1992. Beginning in 1995, Mirsaidov was threatened, and beaten, and his car was bombed. He lived as a target for three years before announcing in 1998 that his organization had failed in its mission to unite opposition groups and had fallen apart. By the end of the year, many leading Uzbek opposition figures were in exile or in prison. A new law passed by the rubber-stamp parliament in 1996 further tightened the noose on potential opposition parties. It banned all parties organized around ethnic or religious interests. In addition, it required that they have at least 5,000 members in eight of Uzbekistan's 12 administrative regions in order to gain official status.

The pattern of repression and arrests continued through the 1990s and into the new decade. Then, on February 16, 1999, a series of bombs exploded in Tashkent, apparently as part of a plot to assassinate Karimov, who escaped unharmed because he was late for a meeting. The blasts killed 15 people and injured more than 120. Karimov blamed what he called "religious fanatics" for the attack and found evidence that the Islamic Movement of Uzbekistan was involved. However, the wave of arrests that followed swept up both Islamic opponents and secular critics of the regime. Two trials quickly followed. In July, six of 22 Islamic militants accused of the crime received death sentences and the rest received prison sentences of eight to 20 years. In August, six more defendants, all members of Erk, received sentences of eight to 12 years.

In January 2000, President Karimov's first term finally ended and Uzbekistan held a new election. It was a two-man race, with Karimov running against the leader of the PDPU, Abdulhafiz Jalalov, who outside the polling station where he voted announced that he had voted for Karimov in the interest of "order and internal peace." Jalalov nonetheless managed to win 4.2 percent of the vote, well short of the 91.9 percent received by the victorious Karimov. The Organization for Security and Cooperation in Europe and other international organizations concerned with promoting democracy refused Uzbekistan's offer to monitor the elections on the grounds that the voters clearly were not being allowed to participate in a genuine election. Just short of two years later, in November 2001, more than 90 percent of Uzbekistan's voters dutifully came to the polls in yet another referendum to approve a constitutional amendment to extend the presidential term to December 2007. This was another example of what Karimov called "democracy, Uzbek style." A representative of the international organization Human Rights Watch saw it differently, commenting that under the current conditions in Uzbekistan "there is no possibility for any free or fair vote, or for an informed choice to be made at the ballot box."

A NEW UZBEK HISTORY

Repression was one tool the Karimov regime used to forge a united Uzbekistan. It also promoted Uzbek national identity by rewriting history. The Bashmachis, who had fought Soviet rule and therefore had been

The Amir Timur Museum in Tashkent was rushed to completion in time for Tamerlane's 660th birthday. Its exhibits include scale models of his construction projects and manuscripts and engravings from his time. (AI Photo, Uzbekistan)

depicted negatively before 1991, were transformed into Uzbek patriots. Suddenly, a national past miraculously stretched back centuries earlier than previously realized to at least the first century B.C. Tamerlane, who during the Soviet era had been pictured as a destructive marauder—his military campaigns and brutality have been blamed for as many as 17 million deaths—was transformed by Karimov's historians into a just ruler and symbol of national pride. In 1993 Karimov dedicated a huge bronze statue to Tamerlane in central Tashkent where once a statue of Soviet hero Karl Marx had stood. Elsewhere in Uzbekistan, the man many people called Amir Timur, or Timur the Great, was honored in public places with statues, busts, and portraits. In 1996, a new museum opened in Tashkent to chronicle the conqueror's achievements. By the end of the decade streets, markets, and calendars all bore his name, as did a brand of cigarettes. Kiosks throughout the country were selling a pocketbook of selected quotes called *Utterances of Amir Timur.* Only Karimov himself was more omnipresent. Karimov used Tamerlane's conquests to justify his efforts to increase Uzbekistan's influence over its Central Asian neighbors. Yet not everyone was impressed. In 1998, a 17-year-old girl selling souvenirs in front of Tamerlane's tomb in Samarkand told an Associated Press reporter: "All we hear nowadays is Timur, Timur, Timur. I don't know what to make of him. I only know that they just tore down 16 or 18 houses here to build a Timur fountain, and that's bad."

As Tamerlane's role in Uzbek history waxed, that of the Soviet Union waned. By 2002, the term "Soviet" was banned. A government decree required schools and libraries to remove textbooks and training manuals printed before 1993, an order that in practice proved impossible to carry out completely because of the severe shortage of textbooks. Foreign medical and language textbooks also fell victim to the new campaign. The volumes removed from the shelves of schools and libraries were sent for pulping and turned into toilet paper. The effort to build up Uzbek history and culture extended to music. The state's music schools were told to eliminate the works of the European composers Mozart, Bach, and Beethoven because, the government claimed, "Uzbekistan has plenty of great composers of its own." Lest anyone be confused about the extent of Uzbekistan's greatness, a new monument in central Tashkent removed all doubt. Nicknamed by local people the "globe of Uzbekistan," it was a huge stone globe representing the world mounted on a pedestal. The outline of one country—Uzbekistan—covered almost half the globe.

THE CHALLENGE OF ISLAMIC FUNDAMENTALISM

It was Islamic fundamentalist groups rather than secular or democratic forces that provided the only effective sustained opposition to the Karimov regime. The end of Soviet-imposed atheism led to a surge of interest in Islam throughout Uzbekistan. Between 1991 and 1997, the number of mosques in the country rose from 80 to more than 5,000. While the Karimov government could do nothing to stop this development, it did try to promote moderate rather than militant views of Islam. It sponsored state-controlled Islamic schools and arrested or removed Muslim clerics who preached militant ideas. Students studying Islam abroad were called home to keep them from being exposed to fundamentalist ideas spreading throughout the Muslim world, often financed by money from Saudi Arabia. These efforts against militant Islam intensified in 1996 when the fundamentalist Taliban movement overran most of Afghanistan,

Uzbekistan's southern neighbor. Between 1998 and 2001, the Karimov regime imprisoned more than 7,000 people it accused of membership in fundamentalist organizations trying to overthrow the government. It used brutal torture to get the prisoners to confess. Often those people were not militants but simply devout Muslims who had chosen to worship elsewhere than in state-controlled mosques.

For several years the most dangerous Islamic fundamentalist group opposing Karimov, and the largest such group in Central Asia, was the Islamic Movement of Uzbekistan (IMU), a terrorist organization founded by Uzbek exiles based in Taliban-controlled Afghanistan. Its spiritual leader was Tohir Yuldeshev, an Islamic preacher, or mullah, from the Fergana Valley. Yuldeshev was strongly influenced by Wahhabi doctrines that had originated in Saudi Arabia. The group's top military commander, Juma Namangani, also came from the Fergana Valley. He had learned his military skills in the late 1980s when he was drafted into the Soviet army and sent to fight in Afghanistan. At the time, the Soviet Union was trying to help the Communist Afghan government defeat Islamic guerrillas, an effort that ultimately failed. Yuldeshev and Namangani formed the IMU in 1998 with the goal of establishing an Islamic state in Uzbekistan based on the *sharia*, or Islamic law. In announcing their goal they also proclaimed a jihad, or Islamic holy war, against the Karimov government.

The IMU initially enjoyed success, in part because of outside help. The militant Islamic Taliban government in Afghanistan gave the IMU military aid and safe bases from which to operate, while Osama bin Laden's terrorist organization, al-Qaeda, provided financial help. The IMU's forces, numbering about 1,500 at their peak, were active in Tajikistan and Kyrgyzstan as well as in Uzbekistan. In 2000, the IMU launched major guerrilla attacks in both Uzbekistan and Kyrgyzstan. Islamic guerrillas entered Uzbekistan from bases in Tajikistan outfitted with modern equipment such as night-vision goggles. They killed dozens of people in fighting that came to within 60 miles (100 km) of Tashkent, Uzbekistan's capital. Then the IMU's fortunes changed for the worse. On September 11, 2001, al-Qaeda terrorists destroyed New York City's World Trade Center, killing close to 3,000 people. The United States responded by attacking Afghanistan, routing the Taliban and destroying much of bin Laden's terror network. The IMU thus lost its main sources of support outside Uzbekistan. Namangani, whose military skills and personal charisma were essential to the IMU's success, reportedly was killed by an American air strike in November 2001, and by 2002 the organization appeared to be in decline. However, by the end of the year there were reports that the IMU was regrouping and possibly cooperating with other militant Islamic groups.

The decline of the IMU left a secretive group called Hizb-ut-Tahrir (Party of Islamic Liberation, or HT) as the leading Islamic fundamentalist organization in Uzbekistan. It was founded in Saudi Arabia and Jordan in 1953 by a Palestinian cleric and reached Uzbekistan in the mid-1990s. Its goal is to bring all of Central Asia and the entire Islamic world under the rule of a single Islamic state governed according to the *sharia*. It then intends to spread Islam to the rest of the world by jihad, or holy war, training and conscripting all Muslim men over the age of 15 for that effort. Its model for how to govern is the caliphate, the state that ruled the Muslim world in the seventh century. Hizb-ut-Tahrir rejects democracy—an Islamic council with dictatorial powers would govern its caliphate—as well as capitalism and socialism. All are considered Western concepts alien to Islam. Operating in small cells of five to seven men, by 2001 HT had become the largest underground movement not only in Uzbekistan, but also in Tajikistan and Kyrgyzstan. Mass arrests certainly had not succeeded in breaking its organization in Uzbekistan, where according to well-informed observers more than 5,100 of the country's 7,600 political prisoners belonged to HT. Another 1,600 belonged to the IMU.

Caught in the middle of the struggle between a secular dictatorial government and would-be dictatorial Islamic fundamentalists, who would have been more tyrannical than Karimov, were the ordinary citizens of Uzbekistan. On the one hand, many people feared the government and felt helpless in the face of repression and economic hard times. As one teacher told a Western journalist in the spring of 2001, "Families live with their heads down struggling to survive. . . . We can't eat ideals and slogans any more. Things are getting desperate for everyone." On the other hand, there often was little sympathy for the Islamic fundamentalists, especially among educated Uzbek citizens. As one airline employee told a Western reporter, "I'm glad Karimov is locking these Wahhabis up. They are a menace to society." His wife, an economist, added, "Don't get me wrong. I'm not against religion. I'm a believer. I just don't think I need to be covered from head to toe in a *burka** to prove it. It's like anything else in life, moderation is best."

The Economy

Uzbekistan's economy declined by about 18 percent between 1991 and 1995. While this was a painful fall, it was less than half of the loss suffered by its neighbors Kazakhstan and Kyrgyzstan and by many other former Soviet republics. Uzbekistan's relatively moderate losses were due in part to good luck and high world prices for cotton and gold, two of its most important exports.

The state kept a tight grip on the economy. This probably helped the transition from a planned to a free market economy, at least in the short run. Businesses that otherwise would have failed were kept open, and many social services from the Soviet era were at least partially maintained. At the same time, control over the economy strengthened the autocratic power of the Karimov regime and fed corruption that already was widespread.

Despite the generally slow pace toward a free market economy, houses and small businesses were privatized. By 1995, according to government statistics, more than two-thirds of Soviet-era state enterprises were in private hands. Appearance, however, did not always reflect reality. The right personal connections rather than good business practices were the keys to success in business in Uzbekistan. In agriculture, Soviet-era farms controlled by the state officially were converted into cooperatives. Yet the farmers who suddenly became members of cooperatives were not permitted to sell their shares. The state also continued to buy, and therefore control, the bulk of the country's cotton and wheat crops, Uzbekistan's two most important agricultural products. Some private farms were established, but the state owned the land on which private farmers worked. One positive development was the attempt to diversify agriculture by raising more food crops. The main focus was on growing more wheat. While the acreage sown for cotton declined slightly, for wheat it was increased by 50 percent.

---

*A *burka* is a garment worn by women in traditional Islamic societies that covers their bodies from head to toe.

Meanwhile, large economic enterprises remained almost entirely state-owned. Ten years after independence, one expert described the pace of large enterprise privatization as "glacially slow." While this discouraged investment from foreign firms, some industries in the mining and energy sectors of the economy did attract foreign investors. Foreign firms also invested in Uzbekistan's automobile industry, the most important manufacturing industry the country inherited from the Soviet era. Foreign investors formed joint ventures with an association of Uzbek companies called Uzavtosaonat, set up by the government in 1994. Its most important joint venture was with the Korean company Daewoo, which built a $640 million factory in the Fergana Valley that opened in 1996. By 2002, it was producing 200,000 cars per year. In another venture, a Turkish company opened a factory in Samarkand in 1999 to produce 5,000 minibuses and trucks per year. German firms also invested in the Uzbek auto industry, as did the U.S. firm Exide, which at the end of 2002 had a 51 percent share in a new factory slated to produce 1 million automobile batteries per year.

Despite many problems, Uzbekistan's economy began to grow in 1996. By the year 2000, it had recovered to its 1991 level, and it grew by 4.5 percent in 2001. Still, the bad news for Uzbekistan's economy outweighed the good. Cotton remained the country's most important export, which meant that Uzbekistan's economy remained hostage to the world price for that single crop. Despite a decade of effort, the country was not self-sufficient in wheat or in other foods. While government controls had helped stabilize the economy, those controls and the failure to privatize large industries, coupled with corruption, remained a major barrier to foreign investment. Foreign investment in turn was essential to modernizing the economy. The prospect for the economy as a whole over the long term seemed weighted more toward stagnation than modernization and growth.

Uzbekistan and the World

During its first decade of independence, Uzbekistan gradually began to compete with Russia for influence in Central Asia. This was not entirely surprising. Uzbekistan was the most populous country in the region.

Russia's international power was only a shadow of what the former Soviet Union had known. What is more surprising was that Uzbekistan became a security partner of the United States. That partnership grew out of the conquest of most of Afghanistan by the Taliban. After coming to power in the mid-1990s, the Taliban gave refuge to Osama bin Laden and his terrorist organization al-Qaeda. When al-Qaeda terrorists destroyed the World Trade Center in September 2001, the United States concluded that in order to destroy al-Qaeda it had to first drive the Taliban from power. That required military bases near Afghanistan, and one of the best locations available was southern Uzbekistan, which borders northern Afghanistan. Soon U.S. troops were in Uzbekistan. In late 2001, an American military assault, assisted by local Afghans, drove the Taliban from power. But the United States was unable to completely destroy either the Taliban or al-Qaeda, which meant it still needed bases in Uzbekistan to continue the hunt. As of early 2002, the United States had

Uzbekistan has provided assistance to the United States in its effort to wipe out terrorists based in Afghanistan. In March 2002 Presidents Islam Karimov and George W. Bush shook hands in the White House after signing agreements dealing with a variety of issues. (AI Photo, Uzbekistan)

THE WORLD'S MOST RIDICULOUS BORDERS

"People are trapped. They cannot travel, cannot trade, cannot create business," a human rights activist in Bishkek told a Western journalist in May 2002. She was referring to people in the Fergana Valley who live in patches of Uzbekistan, Kyrgyzstan, and Tajikistan that are completely surrounded by foreign territory. These enclaves are the result of borders drawn during the Soviet era. They had little practical meaning at the time because all of Central Asia belonged to one country. But when the Soviet regime fell, what had been lines on a Soviet map became international borders. Residents who routinely had traveled from village to village on business or for personal reasons suddenly had to stop for hours at border posts, waiting to get their visas stamped or to pay bribes to cross from one country into another. Daily life was badly disrupted, and people, unable to do business or visit friends and family, suffered financially and personally. Matters worsened after 1999, when Uzbekistan tightened its border controls after bombings in Tashkent that were blamed on the Islamic Movement of Uzbekistan. Barbed-wire fences cut villages off from schools, markets, and other vital resources. Irrigation channels were cut or diverted, denying people access to vital sources of water. Some of the fences ran right through the center of villages.

Two of the major Fergana Valley enclaves belong to Uzbekistan, both surrounded by Kyrgyz territory. Sokh, the largest, has an area of about 325 square miles and a population of about 43,000. Virtually surrounded by barbed wire, it is about 25 miles (40 km) from Uzbekistan proper. Complicating matters even more, ethnic Tajiks make up 99 percent of its population. Not far to the east is Shakhimardan, another Uzbek enclave. Its population is 91 percent Tajik. West of Sokh, also surrounded by Kyrgyz territory, is the Vorukh enclave, which belongs to Tajikistan. It has a population, almost all Tajik, of 25,000. The remaining smaller enclaves include a Kyrgyz village surrounded by Uzbek territory, two specks of Uzbek territory in Kyrgyzstan, and two tiny pieces of Tajikistan, one in Uzbekistan and the other in Kyrgyzstan.

The Fergana Valley borders make life difficult even for people who do not live in the enclaves. Before 1991, it took about an hour to travel between the southern Kyrgyz cities of Osh and Jalalabad. Now it takes four hours, either via the direct route through Uzbek territory and border checkpoints or via winding side roads. Given the political realities of the region, any possible solution to these problems lies years in the future.

1,500 troops deployed at a former Soviet air base in southern Uzbekistan. In March of that year, Uzbekistan and the United States signed a military agreement. The United States pledged its support for Uzbekistan's security and territorial integrity and agreed to aid Uzbekistan in carrying out internal reforms, including political reforms that would promote democracy. In 2002, that aid was $160 million, most of which was going to train and equip Uzbek police and soldiers. This aid could be expected to help the Uzbeks combat the drug trade and secure their borders against Islamic militants. Aid from the United States, however, was very unlikely to change the dictatorial nature of the Karimov regime.

NOTES

p. 114 " 'We travel not for trafficking alone: . . .' " Quoted in Calum MacLeod and Bradley Mayhew, *Uzbekistan: The Golden Road to Samarkand.* (Hong Kong: Odyssey Publications, 1999), p. 149.

p. 114 " 'the noblest public square in the world.' " Quoted in Michael Mewshaw, "Uzbekistan's Golden City," *The New York Times Magazine,* March 3, 1996, p. 27.

p. 119 " 'We have not had enough water for three years . . .' " Quoted in Elena Dubrovskaya, "Agricultural Crisis Prompts Uzbek Officials to Revive Interest in Plan to Divert Siberian Rivers." 1 July 2002. Eurasianet. Available on-line. URL: http://www. eurasianet.org/departments/environment/articles/eav052002. shtml Downloaded July 1, 2002, p. 1.

p. 125 " 'order and internal peace.' " Quoted in *The Jamestown Foundation Monitor,* January 13, 2000.

p. 125 " 'democracy, Uzbek style.' " Quoted in *The Boston Globe,* November 6, 2001, p. A3.

p. 125 " 'there is no possibility for any free or fair vote, . . .' " *The Boston Globe,* November 6, 2001, p. A3.

p. 127 " 'All we hear nowadays is Timur, Timur, Timur . . .' " Quoted in "Uzbek Despot Labeled a Hero." www.th-record.com1998/01/1-5-98/tamerl.htm Downloaded October 17, 2002.

p. 127 " 'Uzbekistan has plenty of grat composers of its own.' " Igor Rotar, Quoted in "Myths and Prejudice Across the FSU," *Russia and Eurasia Review* (The Jamestown Foundation, December 17, 2002), p. 3.

p. 129 " 'Families live with their heads down . . .' " Quoted in Jennifer Balfour, "The Crisis Facing Uzbek Youth Today," April 4, 2001. Eurasianet. Available on-line. URL:http://www.eurasianet.org/departments/insight/articles/eav040401. shtml Downloaded July 1, 2002, p. 2.

pp. 129–130   " 'I'm glad Karimov is locking these Wahhabis up. . . .' " Quoted in Mathew Brzezinski, "Whatever It Takes," *The New York Times Sunday Magazine*, December 16, 2001, p.76.

p. 131   " 'glacially slow Richard Pomfret,' " "Recent Economic Reforms in Uzbekistan. Central Asia-Caucasus Analyst, Weekly Briefing, September 26, 2001. Available on-line. URL:http://www.cornellcaspian.com/analyst/010926_H1htm. Downloaded October 18, 2002.

p. 133   " 'People are trapped. They cannot travel, . . .' " Quoted in *The New York Times*, May 21, 2002, p. A8.

9

TURKMENISTAN

Turkmenistan is a poverty-stricken country with a tyrannical govern-ment. It also has natural resources that have the potential to make it rich. Made up largely of vast, inhospitable deserts, during the Soviet era it attracted little outside attention. That indifference turned to interest when the Soviet Union collapsed and Turkmenistan became an inde-pendent country in the waning days of 1991. Suddenly the world's fifth-largest natural gas reserves under Turkmenistan's desert sands and beneath the waters of its share of the Caspian Sea were free from Moscow's control and potentially open to development by energy com-panies from the industrialized world. Significant oil reserves further enhanced Turkmenistan's potential importance to foreign investors and governments. As the last decade of the 20th century began, Turk-menistan's enormous energy resources had made the country impossible to ignore the country any longer.

A Country Map

Turkmenistan, the southern-most of the former Soviet republics, covers an area of 188,500 square miles (488,100 sq km), about the size of Cal-ifornia and South Carolina combined. Like Kazakhstan, Turkmenistan looks a bit like a tank, only less than one-fifth the size of its giant northern neighbor and facing in the opposite direction, its turret pointed toward the east. Turkmenistan's longest border is a 1,007-mile

(1,621-km) frontier with Uzbekistan to the north and northeast. A 235-mile border in the northwest separates Turkmenistan from Kazakhstan. Turkmenistan has a 616-mile (992-km) border with Iran to the southwest and a 462-mile (744-km) border with Afghanistan to the southeast. Due west is Turkmenistan's 1,098-mile (1,768-km) Caspian Sea coastline. Part of that coastline loops around Garabogaz Bay, a 7,000-square mile (18,100-sq km) inlet that really is the world's largest lagoon. The bay is almost completely cut off from the main body of the Caspian Sea by a sliver of land about 40 miles long, split in two by a narrow strait that in some places is only about 1,600 feet wide. Its shallow waters are much saltier than those of the Caspian Sea and almost as salty as the ocean. Turkmenbashi (formerly Krasnovodsk), the country's main port, is on a peninsula just south of the bay. The Garagum (Black Sands) Desert, where shifting winds create sand mountains more than 60 feet high and several miles in length, covers about 80 percent of the country. The Garagum and other desert regions in Turkmenistan are expanding, as are deserts elsewhere in Central Asia. The main relief from Turkmenistan's desert landscape is in the south, where the Köpetdag mountains form a natural border with Iran. The mountains stand on shifting plates in the earth's crust that make the region an earthquake zone. In 1948, a powerful earthquake demolished Ashgabat (population 525,000) and killed more than 100,000 people. There are smaller mountains along Turkmenistan's border with Kazakhstan. Most of the population lives in oasis settlements near the country's few sources of freshwater.

The Amu Darya is Turkmenistan's most important river. It enters the eastern part of the country from Afghanistan, becomes part of the Turkmenistan-Uzbekistan border, and then flows completely into Uzbekistan along its course toward the Aral Sea. The Murgap River, a much smaller stream, enters southeastern Turkmenistan from Afghanistan and flows northward until it disappears into the country's desert sands. The Mugap's waters fill the Sary Yazy, the largest of the country's 11 reservoirs. Turkmenistan's other major waterway is the Soviet-built Garagum Canal, which runs from the Amu Darya for 900 miles (1,448 km) across the desert as it irrigates the country's enormous cotton fields. Along the way the canal loses about half its water. Leakage from the Garagum and other canals has created more than 2 million acres of useless salt marshes in Turkmenistan's deserts. Meanwhile the Aral Sea to the north has been starved of water, and only about 3 percent of the country's land is actually irrigated. The most visible product of wasteful irrigation is Lake Saryqamysh in the north along the border with Uzbekistan. Most of the lake, formed by agricultural water runoff that collected in a subsea-level desert depression, is in Turkmenistan. Almost all of the fish living in its polluted waters are unfit for human consumption.

The disastrous consequences of the Soviet-era irrigation projects have not dissuaded President Niyazov from planning an even larger scheme: a plan to create a 1,540-square-mile (4,000-sq. km) sea in the middle of the Garagum Desert with the goal of meeting Turkmenistan's growing water requirements for the next 50 years. Niyazov approved the project in 2000 at a projected cost of $4.5 billion and immediately allocated $37.8 million for 100 bulldozers and 160 earth excavators to be bought in Japan. The project is to be funded by a specially formed Lake of the Golden Century Organization.

CLIMATE

Most of Turkmenistan has a subtropical desert climate. Summers are long and very hot, with temperatures in the Garagum Desert often reaching 122°F (50°C) during the day. Winters are short and much cooler. Most of Turkmenistan gets barely three inches (80 mm) of rain per year with the exception of the mountain areas in the south, where average annual rainfall is between 11 and 12 inches (300 mm).

NATURAL RESOURCES

Turkmenistan has enormous natural gas deposits, probably the fifth largest in the world. It also has significant oil deposits. Half of the country's irrigated land is devoted to producing cotton, which has made Turkmenistan the world's 10th-largest cotton producer. Like Uzbekistan, Turkmenistan faces a critical shortage of water. Much of its soil and underground water has been polluted by pesticides and agricultural chemicals as well as by increased salt levels caused by poor irrigation methods.

People

Turkmenistan's population as of mid-2001 was about 4.6 million and was growing at the rate of about 1.85 percent per year. Ethnic Turkmen make up about 77 percent of the population. The main minority groups are Uzbeks (9.2 percent), Russians (6.7 percent), and Kazakhs (2 percent). About 89 percent of the population are Sunni Muslims and about 9 percent are Eastern Orthodox Christians. One of the few positive legacies of the Soviet era is a literacy rate of 98 percent: 99 percent for men and 97 percent for women. About 650,000 Turkmen, the descendants of people who fled Soviet collectivization, live in Afghanistan, and about 1 million live in northern Iran.

CULTURE AND DAILY LIFE

There are few places in Turkmenistan where the people can escape the endless din of propaganda glorifying Saparmurat Niyazov, the country's dictator. The goal of that campaign is to turn Niyazov, a man whose ego far exceeds his talents, into the greatest hero of the Turkmen people. One man who never needed propaganda to become a genuine national icon was Feragi Magtymguly, the national poet of the Turkmen and their most honored literary figure. Magtymguly probably was born in 1733 and died around 1790. His poems were written in simple language and combined traditional Turkmen proverbs and home-spun wisdom with Islamic imagery. Among his themes was Turkmen unity and nationalism, which resonated powerfully at a time of destructive inter-clan warfare. His poetry was beautifully suited to traditional Turkmen music, and many poems became favorites with folk singers who accompanied themselves with a two-stringed instrument called the *dutar*. Magtymguly and his poems remain as popular today as ever with the Turkmen people, who continue to call him "Magtymguly, Bestower of Happiness."

Many old customs are alive and well in Turkmenistan. The elderly are still deeply respected, and youngest sons are expected to stay at home to care for their parents when they reach old age. More Turkmen, both men and women, continue to wear traditional clothing on a daily basis than do people in other Central Asian countries. The male outfit consists of baggy pants stuffed into high boots, heavy silk jackets, and shaggy wool

Ashgabat in the year 2000 was still a city where many of the old ways survived. This vendor, in his traditional shaggy wool hat and silk jacket, is selling his wares in a local market. (AP/Wide World Photos/Alexander Zemlianichenko)

hats. Women wear colorful ankle-length silk dresses over silk trousers. Many marriages are still arranged. Beautiful handmade Turkmen rugs are often still an important part of a bride's dowry. Notwithstanding the country's constitution, which declares that men and women have equal rights, Turkmen tradition governs most marriages, leaving men with the power to make most decisions. Fathers marry off their daughters in order of their age.

While Turkmen eat mutton and other meats, their diet includes many vegetarian dishes, including a meatless *plov* made with dried fruit. Other traditional foods included cornmeal pancakes, flat bread, and a variety of porridges made with various ingredients.

Politics and Government

The story of Turkmenistan's political life since 1991 is the story of the evolution of President Saparmurat Niyazov's personal dictatorship. Born in 1940 and orphaned as a young child, Niyazov rose to leader of the Communist Party of the Turkmen SSR during the Soviet era. He won the post of president in October 1990 in an election in which, running unopposed, he received 98.3 percent of the vote. He soon pushed aside all potential rivals, driving most of them into exile, and established a brutally repressive personal dictatorship. Niyazov was reelected president to a five-year term in 1992 with a reported 99.5 percent of the vote in another election where he appeared alone on the ballot. In a referendum two years later, 99.9 percent of the voters approved extending Niyazov's term by five years to 2002. Electoral support, however, did not satisfy him: In 1999 he had himself declared president for life, the only politician in Central Asia to take that step. That presumably would allow him to rule well into the next century. He told his countrymen that this will be the "Golden Century of the Turkmen."

Turkmenistan has a parliament, but it is a legislature without any power that meets solely to approve Niyazov's decisions. People brave enough to dissent often disappear without a trace or end up in prisons and labor camps. Niyazov's political opponents must go into foreign exile in order to survive. Niyazov has periodically removed officials from office without cause and purged government agencies in order to prevent anyone from gaining enough strength to challenge his rule. In 2002 he thoroughly purged his security apparatus from the top down, allegedly for corruption. The main reason for the purge almost certainly was a series of defections by former top officials, all of whom wisely chose to live abroad.

While nobody inside Turkmenistan dared complain or criticize Niyazov's exercises in self-glorification, Turkmen living outside the country eventually began speaking up.

In June 2002, several of them met in Vienna, Austria, in an attempt to bring the situation in Turkmenistan to the attention of the international community. It was the first time a group of exiled Turkmen dissidents had gotten together to speak to an international audience. The group had some credibility because it included two former foreign ministers, one of whom had broken with Niyazov in late 2001. In what surely was an understatement the group declared. "The cult of personality surrounding him [Niyazov] has reached grotesque proportions." Shirali Nurmuradov, a Turkmen poet living in exile in Sweden, described the situation more graphically. "You know, there is a cult, but no personality,"

TURKMENBASHI: LEADER OF ALL THE TURKMEN

Even by Central Asia's standards of authoritarian rule, Niyazov and the cult of adoration that surrounds him stand out. His system of corrupt personal rule comes closer than any other in the region to being a pure sultanistic regime. Shortly after independence, Niyazov had his rubber-stamp parliament award him a newly created honor called the Order of the Hero of the Turkmen People. In 1993 he gave himself a new and grander title, "Turkmenbashi," or "Leader of All the Turkmen." Soon innumerable places such as streets, schools, public buildings, airports, factories, communal farms, and cities were being named after him, including the Caspian Sea port of Krasnovodsk, which was renamed Turkmenbashi. Pictures and statues of Niyazov were literally every-where. (When he dyed his hair black in 1999, thousands of portraits showing him with graying hair had to be quickly replaced.) Niyazov's portrait was on every denomination of Turkmenistan's currency, as well as on postage stamps, bottles of vodka, and packages of tea. The stat-ues erected in Niyazov's honor—there were more than 2,000 of the president and his family throughout the country by 1999—included a 35-foot, gold-plated likeness atop a 246-foot arch in the capital of Ash-gabat. It rotates once every 24 hours so Turkmenbashi's outstretched arms always extend toward the sun. The statue is illuminated at night by spotlights. Niyazov's birthplace and the school he attended became national shrines, while his deceased mother, one of more than 100,000 people killed in an earthquake that devastated Ashgabat in 1948, has been given saintlike status. Niyazov's book *Rukhnama,* or "Spiritual Revival" (published in 2001 to provide a code of living for all Turkmen), has become required reading in all the country's schools. In many schools it often served as the *only* educational tool. Students have been told they are studying "The *Rukhnama* of President Saparmurat Turk-menbashi the Great." One observer familiar with Turkmenistan's schools, having been guaranteed anonymity, told a Western journalist, "All that happens in school now is singing songs and reading *Rukh-nama.*" In addition, every government office devotes an hour a week to the book. Government officials compared it to the Bible and the Qur'an in importance. Officials working in those offices kiss Turkmenbashi's hand when they greet him. That hand is adorned by two gaudy rings, one holding a huge diamond that a Western journalist estimated "must be on the short list of the world's largest stones," and the other sporting a gigantic sapphire set in diamonds.

Television provided no relief, as most broadcasts on the state-controlled network featured long commentaries by Turkmenbashi on the *Rukhnama.* In 2001, the state-run television channel's most important new program was a new series called "Turkmenbashi, the Patron"; it was a sequel to the 19-episode series, "Turkmenbashi, My Leader." *All* broadcasts, at all times, included a golden silhouette of the president in the upper right-hand corner of the screen. This programming helps to explain why television satellite dishes have sprouted from roofs and windows in the capital of Ashgabat: Regardless of their wealth, many Turkmen eagerly pay for equipment that will bring them broadcasts from Russian television.

Niyazov's lifestyle mirrors his political status. While most Turkmen struggle to get by on incomes of about $15 to $20 per month, Niyazov lives in a specially built, $80 million presidential palace topped by a gold dome. It is only one of many huge and expensive building projects that have changed the face of Ashgabat since 1991. One of them is a massive new cultural palace where visitors pass 35-foot wooden doors and inlaid gold inscriptions of Niyazov's thoughts as they enter the building. Others include a structure billed as the world's largest fountain, a building for the country's powerless parliament, and a new national museum.

In the summer of 2002, Niyazov renamed the days of the week and the months of the year. To no one's surprise, January became Turkmenbashi, while September was renamed Rukhnama. April became Gurbansoltan—actually Gurbansoltan Ije, or "Granny Gurbansoltan"—in honor of Niyazov's mother. Lest anyone miss the point, another of Ashgabat's huge new statues showed a young Gurbansoltan seated atop a globe of the world, itself perched atop a gigantic black granite bull, holding up a golden statue of Turkmenbashi as a child. At the country's supreme court, beneath a portrait of Turkmenbashi himself, a likeness of his mother held the scales of justice before presidential banners. Turkmenbashi's declarations included the welcome news that old age did not begin until age 85.

Nurmuradov told a Western reporter. He then added, "We cannot refer to him [Niyazov] as personality. It's imbecility, and it's progressing."

In November 2002, gunmen in Ashgabat opened fire on the presidential motorcade in a failed attempt to assassinate Niyazov. He responded with a wave of arrests that targeted the families of exiled opposition leaders, all of whom denied being involved. The government quickly handed down harsh jail sentences and, in early 2003, tightened its control over travel and other activities. Given the failure of the plot, the main hope for change in Turkmenistan probably was Niyazov's health, in particular his heart condition. In 1994 he flew to Texas to have a blood clot removed from his leg. In 1997 Niyazov had quadruple cardiac bypass surgery in Germany, a procedure that kept him out of the country for a month. While he seemed to have recovered, the true state of his health remained uncertain. He ignored warnings by his doctors to follow a strict diet and take his prescribed medicines. Nor was he willing to give up cognac, his favorite alcoholic beverage. In the fall of 2002, Niyazov's German cardiologist and several colleagues traveled to Ashgabat to check on the president's health, sparking new rumors about serious problems. Yet he remained in complete control, leaving Turkmenistan, according to the Organization for Security and Cooperation in Europe, as a country with an "absolute lack of any freedom of expression."

The Economy

As was the case elsewhere in Central Asia, Turkmenistan's economy did not do well during the country's first decade of independence. After 1991 the country's overall economy shrank every year until 1997, a decline that included a steep fall of 17.3 percent in 1994. Only in 1998 did the economy begin to grow. That growth, powered by exports of natural gas and cotton, continued into 2002. However, it did not noticeably help most Turkmen. While President Niyazov lived in luxury, a growing percentage of the country's ordinary people sank deeper into poverty. According to the International Monetary Fund, income per person in late 2001 was half of the level of 10 years earlier, when Turkmenistan already was one of the poorest republics in the Soviet Union. As the "Golden Century of the Turkmen" began, the majority of the country's population lived in poverty. Health care services, the educational system, and other public services were deteriorating. Niyazov's extravagant building projects—among them his presidential palace in the center of Ashgabat, 30 large hotels on the city's outskirts that rarely hosted any guests, and a seven-lane highway connecting the center of the city to the surrounding hills—had left the government with a foreign debt of $2.3 billion.

Most experts agree that Turkmenistan's economic future depends on economic reforms to dismantle the centrally controlled economy inherited from the Soviet era and the development of its natural gas resources. However, as of 2002, few significant economic reforms had occurred. The export of natural gas was limited by pipelines leading out of the landlocked country. When Turkmenistan became independent, all of those pipelines led into Russia, which therefore had a stranglehold on Turkmenistan's natural gas exports. Much of that gas ended up in Ukraine, which for several years during the 1990s was unable to pay for the deliveries. Despite the interest shown by foreign companies in building alternate routes to Western markets, Niyazov refused to make key decisions, especially on a proposed route under the Caspian Sea that would pass through Azerbaijan, Georgia, and Turkey. This route, which had the advantage of bypassing Iran as well as Russia, was strongly supported by the United States. The only new natural gas pipeline built during Turkmenistan's first decade of independence, which began operation in 1998, ran through Iran.

The government did make an effort to diversify the economy, both in terms of industry and agriculture. Under Soviet rule Turkmenistan served primarily as a supplier of raw materials. It therefore had few industries. The most important of these were several oil refineries and factories for producing textiles and processing foods. Efforts to expand the industrial base included encouraging several companies based in Turkey to build 18 large textile plants. By the end of the 1990s, Turkmen workers in those factories, putting in 12- to 16-hour days, earned between $20 to $25 per month. The goods made in those factories were exported to the world with "Made-in-Turkey" labels. In agriculture, a serious effort was made to expand wheat production by increasing the amount of land used for providing wheat at the expense of cotton. Despite several years of drought at the turn of the century, that effort succeeded in making Turkmenistan self-sufficient in grain.

Aside from cotton and wheat, by far the country's most important crops, Turkmenistan's farmers also produce melons, grapes, and a variety of vegetables. Animal husbandry, another traditional occupation, also continues to play a small but significant part in Turkmenistan's economy. Karakul sheep are raised to supply wool for Turkmenistan's famous carpets, many of which are manufactured on home looms rather than in the country's carpet factories. One place to buy those carpets is in the outskirts of Ashgabat at the Tolkuchka market, the largest bazaar in Central Asia, where items for sale range from camels and local produce to jewelry and elaborately designed handmade cotton cloth. Not surprisingly, the world's largest hand-woven rug, measuring more than 3,300 square feet, hangs in one of President Niyazov's palaces. Befitting its size and its owner, it has been named "The Golden Age of the Great Saparmurat Turkmenbashi." Among Turkmenistan's most important animals, for symbolic rather than economic reasons, are the Akhal-Teke horses, an ancient breed that nearly became extinct during the Soviet era. Known for their beauty and speed since ancient times, the Akhal-Teke are considered by many experts to be the ancestors of modern thoroughbred racehorses. Regional tradition holds that Alexander the Great rode an Akhal-Teke into battle. Today a state-run ranch devoted to breeding and raising these horses is located about six miles (10 km) from Ashgabat. It is known as the Turkmenbashi Stud Farm.

Turkmenistan and the World

President Niyazov has decreed that Turkmenistan will play a neutral role in world affairs. He underlined that point by calling the arch in Ashgabat on which his rotating statute stands the "Arch of Neutrality." Unlike Kazakhstan, Uzbekistan, and Kyrgyzstan, Turkmenistan refused to get involved in Tajikistan's civil war and did not contribute troops to the Russian-led multinational peacekeeping forces. When the United States attacked Afghanistan in response to the destruction of the World Trade Center in New York City by al-Qaeda terrorists based in that country, Niyazov did not permit U.S. troops to enter Turkmenistan. His only concession to the U.S. anti-terrorism campaign was to allow the United Nations to run relief programs from Turkmen territory. Meanwhile,

No monument better symbolizes the personality cult of Turkmenistan's Saparmurat Niyazov than the huge Arch of Neutrality in Ashgabat, pictured here in 2000. (AP/Wide World Photos/Alexander Zemlianichenko)

Niyazov does everything he can to isolate Turkmenistan's population from the outside world. There are no privately owned or independent newspapers, or radio or television stations. The state-controlled media provides no information about the world at large. Roads are regularly patrolled by police who take down the name of every citizen and register every car they find. Phone calls abroad must be registered 24 hours in advance. And while some citizens of Turkmenistan have satellite dishes that bring them some information from the outside world, very few of them have access to the Internet.

NOTES

p. 141 "'The cult of personality surrounding him . . .'" Quoted in Rustem Safranov, "The World Hears a Unified Turkmen Opposition." EurasiaNet Recaps. June 24, 2002. Available online. URL:http://www.eurasianet.org/departments/recaps/articles/eav062402.shtml Downloaded July 1, 2002.

p. 142 "'All that happens in school now is . . .'" Quoted in Robert G. Kaiser, "Personality Cult Buoys 'Father of All Turkmen'." July 8, 2002. Available online. URL:http://washingtonpost.com/wp-dyn/articles/A36723-2002Jul17.html Downloaded November 11, 2002.

p. 143 "'must be on the short list of . . .'" Joseph Fitchett, "Cult of the Great Leader Lives on in Turkmenistan," June 8, 2000. *International Herald Tribune*. Available on-line. URL:http://iht.com/IHT? DIPLO?00/jf080800.html. Downloaded November 15, 2002.

p. 144 "'We cannot refer to him as . . .'" Quoted in *The New York Times*, August 11, 2002, Section 1, p. 5.

p. 144 "'absolute lack of any freedom . . .'" *Russia's Week*. July 5, 2002. The Jamestown Foundation. Available online. URL:http://www./jamestown.org. Downloaded May 9, 2002.

10

KYRGYZSTAN

Perched high in the Tien Shan and Pamir mountain ranges, tiny Kyrgyz-stan (pronounced: kir-gi-stan) is a country mired deep in poverty and political instability. In 1991, when the country became independent, there was some hope that under President Askar Akayev's leadership Kyr-gyzstan might develop into what some observers optimistically called Central Asia's "island of democracy." That did not happen. While Kyr-gyzstan still was the least oppressive regime in Central Asia in 2002, it was far from democratic, and the authoritarianism that had developed during the country's first 11 years of independence continued to grow. On the economic front, Kyrgyzstan made the most serious attempt in the region to undertake free market reforms in the 1990s. But those efforts bore lit-tle fruit. They could not prevent a steep economic decline that brought hardship to the great majority of the population. Corruption in virtually every aspect of life added to the burden of getting by on a day-to-day basis. As of 2002, Kyrgyzstan's striking scenic beauty stood in stark contrast to its unsightly and growing political, social, and economic problems.

A Country Map

Kyrgyzstan, the second-smallest state in Central Asia, has an area of 76,600 square miles (198,500 sq km), making it slightly smaller than South Dakota. Extending about 560 miles (900 km) east to west and 255 miles (410 km) north to south, Kyrgyzstan looks a little like the head of a crocodile facing westward whose open jaws have the Fergana Valley in a tight grip. Kyrgyzstan borders with Kazakhstan to the north, China to the east and southeast, Tajikistan to the south and west, and Uzbekistan to the west. About 95 percent of the country is mountainous, the average elevation being about 9,020 feet (2,750 meters) above sea level. Forty percent of the country is more than 9,840 feet (3,000 meters) above sea level. The Tien Shan ("Mountains of Heaven") covers about half the country and includes its highest point, Pobeda (Victory) Peak, 24,404 feet (7,439 m) above sea level. These mountains are also home to one of the world's largest glaciers, the South Inylchek Glacier, a frozen river about 40 miles (62 km) long. The northern fringe of the Pamir Mountains skirts Kyrgyzstan along its southern border with Tajikistan. Altogether, Kyrgyzstan's mountains shelter about 6,500 glaciers, which hold a total of about 23 trillion cubic feet (650 billion cubic meters of water).

Kyrgyzstan's main lowlands are its section of the Fergana Valley in the western part of the country and its north-central and northwestern fringes, where mountains descend before giving way to the steppe of Kazakhstan. Bishkek (population: 600,000), the country's capital and industrial center, is located in the north-central region in a fertile river valley 2,625 feet (800 meters) above sea level, about 20 miles (30 km) from the Kazakh border. The city was founded by the Russians in the 1870s on the site of a fort they had seized in 1862. Russians were a majority there when Kyrgyzstan became independent. The city still retains a Russian cultural atmosphere, even though ethnic Kyrgyz make up slightly more than half its population.

Several of Central Asia's most important rivers rise in the mountains of Kyrgyzstan. The Naryn River, the country's largest, begins in the east and flows westward for most of Kyrgyzstan's length into the Fergana Valley and Uzbekistan. There it meets the Kara Darya, which also rises in Kyrgyzstan, to form the Syr Darya. Seven hydroelectric power stations, which store water for irrigation and provide Kyrgyzstan with more than 93 percent of its electric power, line the course of the Naryn. The largest of those projects created the Toktogul Reservoir, the country's second largest body of water. In 2001, that power station produced 10 billion kilowatt-hours of electricity, enough to light the U.S. city of Seattle and its surrounding area. In the far north, the Chu River is bled by irrigation canals along the Kazakh border before flowing completely out of Kyrgyzstan and disappearing into the arid vastness of the Kazakh steppe.

Almost 2,000 lakes, covering about 2,700 square miles (7,000 sq km), dot Kyrgyzstan. By far the largest is Lake Ysyk Köl ("Warm Lake"), one of the world's largest, deepest, and highest mountain lakes, which alone covers an area of more than 2,300 square miles (6,000 sq km). Located in Kyrgyzstan's northeast corner, the deep-blue lake is in a basin about 5,250 feet (1,600 meters) above sea level and about 2,300 feet (700 meters) deep. Local legend extends Ysyk Köl's depth to the center of the earth. Its name comes from a special characteristic: despite its altitude and the frigid winter temperatures in the surrounding mountains, it never freezes. This is because of the high mineral content of its waters—which are too salty for drinking or irrigation—and underground thermal activity in the region. While dozens of rivers flow into the lake, it has no outlet. For all its beauty, Ysyk Köl is suffering. It has been shrinking, possibly in part because rivers flowing into it are having their waters diverted for irrigation, but probably also due to reasons that are not well understood. Overfishing since the Russian arrival in the mid-19th century has depleted important species native to the lake. Attempts to replenish fish stocks with new species have further harmed the natural balance of the lake's ecosystem. Kyrgyzstan's largest freshwater lake is Lake Song Köl. Surrounded by lush pastures that are a magnet for herders seeking feeding ground for their animals, the lake lies in a plain about 3,000 meters above sea level in the center of the country. Unlike the warm waters of Ysyk Köl, Song Köl's waters are ice cold, so frigid that swimming in them is extremely dangerous even in summer.

One serious problem posed by Kyrgyzstan's geography is that mountains isolate parts of the country from each other. The Tien Shan separates Bishkek and the north from the south. Passes in these mountains, whose peaks soar to almost 23,000 feet, are at about 9,800 feet, making them impassable in winter. Over generations this mighty natural barrier has helped produce noticeable cultural differences between the two regions. Today, northern Kyrgyzstan is highly Russified and secular, while in the south both Uzbek and Islamic influences are strong. Russian often is the preferred language in the north, as opposed to Kyrgyz and sometimes Uzbek in the south. Overall, while Bishkek retains Soviet and Russian influences, the major southern cities of Osh and Jalalabad feel distinctly

Central Asian and Islamic. The tensions caused by these and other cultural contrasts, largely suppressed during the Soviet era, have become increasingly pronounced since 1991, when internal republic borders drawn during the Soviet era became international borders. The new international borders also have affected travel within Kyrgyzstan. The journey between northern and southern Kyrgyzstan by train, along a Soviet-built line, must be made via Uzbek territory. In the south, aside from the complicated border jumble of the Fergana Valley, a strip of Uzbek territory jutting eastward into Kyrgyzstan comes between Osh in the far south and Jalalabad, significantly lengthening the land journey between those two cities.

CLIMATE

The mountain regions of Kyrgyzstan have weather that is cold and wet with heavy winter snowfalls. In the higher altitudes the polar climate creates a permanent snow cover. Precipitation in some mountain areas is almost 80 inches per year (200 cm), far higher than the average of about 15 inches (38 cm) for the country as a whole. Some areas of the country get as little as four inches (10 cm) of rain per year. The climate in the northern foothills around Bishkek is temperate, with rainfall occurring in the spring and early summer. During the winter the region is chilled by cold Siberian winds. The Kyrgyz part of the Fergana Valley has a subtropical climate with hot, dry summers.

NATURAL RESOURCES

Kyrgyzstan's most important natural resource is its fast-flowing rivers, which provide water for much of Central Asia and generate large quantities of hydroelectric power. The country also has substantial gold deposits. Those deposits lie in the Kumtor gold field more than 13,000 feet (4,000 m) above sea level in a remote mountain region in the northeastern part of the country above Lake Ysyk Köl. They therefore were beyond the reach of Soviet mining technology. After independence, a joint venture between the Kyrgyz government and a Canadian corporation finally led to development of the field, estimated to be the eighth largest in the world. The project provided the single largest source of foreign investment in Kyrgyzstan. Production began in 1997, giving the country 800 new jobs and the government a major new source of desperately needed revenue, as it receives more than 70 percent of the profits from the mine. In its first year of production, the mine accounted for almost one-third of Kyrgyzstan's foreign earnings. At the same time, the Kumtor mine has been a serious source of environmental pollution. In 1998 and 1999, for example, trucks carrying cyanide for the mines crashed, dumping their highly poisonous cargo into streams that flow into Lake Ysyk Köl and the Syr Darya River. Kyrgyzstan also has deposits of uranium, tin, mercury, antimony, tungsten, and zinc, as well as small deposits of oil and natural gas. Uranium mining has been another source of extremely dangerous environmental pollution. As a result of Soviet mining, Kyrgyzstan is littered with 49 uranium dumps that hold 145 million tons of radioactive wastes.

ENVIRONMENT

Mining is only one of many causes of environmental damage in Kyrgyzstan. Half of Kyrgyzstan's forests have been cut down in the past 50 years, leading to soil erosion, landslides, and other problems. Attempts at reforestation have had very limited success, with only about 10 percent of newly transplanted saplings surviving in the harsh climate of the mountain regions. Overgrazing has stripped pasture land of its plant cover and led to further soil erosion. Industrial wastes from Soviet-era factories and the overuse of dangerous pesticides, especially DDT, have caused significant pollution. Kyrgyzstan's hydroelectric projects have flooded valuable agricultural land in a country where only about 7 percent of the land is arable in any case. Making matters worse, some of those dams are built in earthquake zones, creating the potential for major floods if a dam should fail in an earthquake. Kyrgyzstan also is plagued by environmental problems whose origins are international in scale. For example, its mountain regions and glaciers, along with cold natural habitats worldwide, are increasingly threatened by global warming.

People

When Kyrgyzstan became independent, only about 52 percent of the population of 4.8 million was ethnic Kyrgyz. Russians, who numbered about 18 percent of the population, were the largest minority, followed by the Uzbeks at about 13 percent, Ukrainians at 2.5 percent, and ethnic Germans at 2.4 percent. Those figures changed significantly over the next decade as Russians, Ukrainians, and Germans emigrated while ethnic Central Asians increased their numbers. By the 1999 census, ethnic Kyrgyz accounted for almost 65 percent of the population. Uzbeks, with 13.8 percent, had become the largest minority, while the Russian share of the population fell to 12.5 percent. Uzbeks were concentrated in the southern part of the country, especially in and around the cities of Osh and Jalalabad in the Kyrgyz part of the Fergana Valley, where they constituted slightly more than a third of the population. As of 1999, only 1 percent of Kyrgyzstan's population was Ukrainian, which was equal to the number of Uighurs and a tenth of a percent less than the number of Dugans (ethnic Chinese Muslims). Most ethnic Germans were gone, their share of the total population falling to 0.4 percent. About 70 small ethnic groups, including Kazakhs, Tatars, and Tajiks (each about 0.9 percent), accounted for the rest of the population. Most of Kyrgyzstan's remaining European population lives in Bishkek and the surrounding Chu Valley, the most modern part of the country and where they therefore have the most economic opportunities.

During Kyrgyzstan's first decade of independence, President Akayev, concerned that his country was losing many of its most technically skilled and educated people, made several attempts to keep Russians from emigrating. He focused on the status of the Russian language, an issue of deep concern to the country's Russian community. In 1993, that community was upset when Kyrgyzstan's new constitution made Kyrgyz the official state language. In 1994, a year in which an estimated 100,000 Russians left Kyrgyzstan, Akayev issued a decree to make Russian an official language in areas where Russian speakers predominated. This decree was endorsed by the country's Constitutional Court in 1996. In May 2000, with large-scale Russian emigration unchecked, Russian became Kyrgyzstan's second official language.

Kyrgyzstan's Uzbek community presented a different problem. The Uzbek population was growing and its leaders were demanding more political power, which in turn intensified long-standing Uzbek-Kyrgyz tensions. The Uzbeks claimed, with some justification, that they were underrepresented in Kyrgyzstan's political life, even in parts of Osh and Jalalabad provinces, where they constituted a majority. For example, while ethnic Uzbeks made up more than a quarter of the population of Osh province, in the mid-1990s less than 5 percent of all regional officials were Uzbeks. By mid-2002, the Uzbek agenda was expanding in scope. Citing the elevation of Russian to a state language in 2000, many Uzbeks wanted a constitutional amendment to make Uzbek a state language on a par with Kyrgyz. This in turn raised fears in many Kyrgyz political circles that the next step would be to demand local autonomy in Uzbek areas of the south and possibly even secession from Kyrgyzstan.

As of 2002, about 60 percent of Kyrgyzstan's 4.9 million people lived in rural areas. The country's largest cities were Bishkek (population about 600,000) and Osh (population about 225,000). About 80 percent of the population was Sunni Muslim. Russian Orthodoxy was the country's second-leading faith, although there were no official post-independence figures on the size of that community. Kyrgyzstan also was home to small Catholic, Protestant, Buddhist, and Jewish communities.

CULTURE AND DAILY LIFE

A number of things distinguish daily life in Kyrgyzstan from daily life elsewhere in Central Asia. Perhaps the most notable involves women, who enjoy more freedom than those in neighboring countries, with the possible exception of Kazakhstan. This is in part the result of the Kyrgyz attitude toward Islam: Nomadic Kyrgyz tribesmen historically took a moderate approach toward Islam and did not let it interfere with many pre-Islamic customs and traditions. The status of women in Kyrgyz society was further improved by the secular government policies during the Soviet era. As a result, even Kyrgyz women in rural areas talk freely with men. Women also are allowed to ride alone on the steppe, another unusual custom in Central Asia. Kyrgyz women participate more actively in business, education, and other professions than do women in Uzbekistan, Turkmenistan, or Tajikistan. They even make up one-third of all their country's elected officials, although almost exclusively at the lower levels. At the same time, old traditions that subordinate women to men persist, especially in rural areas. They include the custom of "bride napping," in which young women are kidnaped by a male suitor and held overnight at the home of his parents. Although nothing takes place, the mere fact of spending a night at a man's house often is shameful enough

THE *MANAS* EPIC

Oh, oh, oh, the ancient fairy tale
It is high time to begin it.
The fairy tale of the olden times
It is just time to remember it.
We will speak much
For fearless Manas's sake
For the sake of Manas's memory.

In 1995, with support from the United Nations, Kyrgyzstan staged a three-day festival celebrating the 1,000th anniversary of *Manas,* the epic poem that is the national work of literature of the Kyrgyz people. The *Manas* epic has its origins in the ninth century when the Kyrgyz tribes, living in what today is southern Siberia, defeated powerful invaders from the east and established an independent state. The poem credits the victory to the mythical folk hero Manas, whose strength, bravery, and military skill are virtues the Kyrgyz greatly admire. Legend attributes the origins of the *Manas* epic itself to one of the great hero's 40 elite warriors who, it is said, was a gifted poet.

The epic's real authors actually were illiterate wandering bards known as *manaschi* who recited the saga of Manas's heroic struggle to secure a homeland for his people at festivals or other occasions. They often embellished the story as they went along, incorporating into their performances the triumphs of actual military leaders and attributing these additional heroic exploits to the mythical Manas. Over time the *Manas* evolved into one of the world's most stirring oral poems, the longest poem ever composed, more than five times the combined length of the great Greek epics *The Iliad* and *The Odyssey.* The poem is a trilogy, each part dealing respectively with the exploits of Manas, his son Semetei, and his grandson Seitek. More than a historical narrative, the *Manas* epic encompasses every aspect of the life of the Kyrgyz people, from their struggles and hardships to their customs, ideals, and aspirations. It is the basis of the Kyrgyz claim to be the poets and artists

to force a young woman to accept marriage, something that is deeply resented by young up-to-date Kyrgyz women.

The Kyrgyz also enjoy literary distinction: Chingiz Aitmatov, the only current Central Asian writer with a genuine international reputation. Ait-

of Central Asia. At a time when the Kyrgyz people are going through a difficult period of nation building, President Akayev has invoked the Manas epic as a source of national resolve, calling it "our spiritual foundation, our pride, our strength, and our hope."

Sitting cross-legged in long traditional Kyrgyz robes and white felt hats, *manaschi* sang their individual versions of the poem to the accompaniment of a *komuz,* the traditional Kyrgyz three-stringed musical instrument. Their audience encircled them. The melody gave the poem its distinctive rhythmic basis, which evokes the rhythm of galloping horses that are so central to Kyrgyz life. Manaschi occupied an honored place in Kyrgyz society. One did not choose the profession; rather, it was believed that children were called to it when visited in a dream by Manas's spirits. Parts of the great poem, which existed orally in many versions sung by generations of *manaschi,* were written down for the first time in the 1850s by a pioneering Kazakh anthropologist named Chokan Valikhanov, who called it "the *Iliad* of the steppe." Currently there are more than 60 written versions of *Manas* on record at Kyrgyzstan's National Academy of Sciences. Of these, the one by a *manaschi* named Sagymbai Orozbakov (1894–1930) often receives the highest praise from experts. (It is the version from which the excerpt at the beginning of this feature is taken.) Shortly before his death, Orozbakov allowed recordings of his performances, although they only include the first part of the trilogy. The version that is considered most complete belongs to another outstanding *manaschi,* Sayakbai Karalaev (1894–1971). His version runs more than 500,000 lines and contains references to 113 countries, nations, or tribes and 530 towns, villages, rivers, and geographic regions. The *Manas* epic has commanded such reverence among the Kyrgyz people over many generations that an 18th-century manaschi named Keldybek could confidently begin his performances with a bold injunction and prediction:

> Let the shepherds come and hear me. Their sheep and horses will go home by themselves. Nobody—neither wolf, nor panther, nor thief—will carry off a single lamb while I sing about Manas.

matov was born in 1928, and therefore lived through some of the worst Soviet oppression under Stalin. His novels, stories, and plays, written in both Kyrgyz and Russian, have been translated into English, German, and French. After Stalin's death, Aitmatov wrote works that were acceptable to the Soviet regime, but also some that were so critical that they were banned. One of his best works, *The White Steamship* (1970), mourns the disappearance of traditional myths and folktales—in other words, traditional Kyrgyz culture—under the impact of modern urban life. Aitmatov's best-known novel, *A Day Lasts More Than a Thousand Years* (1980), looks favorably at traditional Central Asian customs. It strongly implies that the Soviet regime was depriving the Central Asians of their cultures, languages, and historical memory, and thereby was turning them into slaves. Aitmatov played an active role in promoting reform during the last years of the Soviet era. Since independence, he has tried to walk the fine line of being a critic of the undemocratic practices of the Akayev regime while at the same time cooperating with it. He was elected to the Kyrgyz parliament in 1995 and as of 2002 was Kyrgyzstan's ambassador to the European Union.

Kyrgyz food, with its emphasis on meat, rice, spices, milk and milk products, and tea, is similar to what is eaten elsewhere in Central Asia.

Round unleavened bread called nan is popular throughout Central Asia. It is often sold in open-air markets, such as this one in downtown Bishkek. (AP/Wide World Photos/Misha Japaridze)

However, the Kyrgyz ignore the Muslim ban on alcoholic beverages, enjoying both their native fermented drinks (the most popular made from mare's milk) and Russian vodka. While some Kyrgyz, especially in rural areas, wear traditional clothing that includes baggy leather trousers, sheepskin coats, and coarse shirts for both men and women, Western-style clothing is worn more widely than in most of the rest of Central Asia.

Politics and Government

Since 1991, Kyrgyzstan's political life has slid toward authoritarian rule mixed with infighting and corruption. In October 1991, running unopposed, Akayev was elected president of Kyrgyzstan with 95 percent of the vote. Much of the early infighting involved the president's reform program. It included political reforms as well as the dismantling of the centrally planned socialist economy inherited from the Soviet era, replacing it with a free market economy. As Akayev put it in December 1991, Kyrgyzstan's progress depended on "the development of private interest, private life, and private property." Despite apparent public support for his programs, Akayev ran into opposition in the parliament. That opposition was centered in the Kyrgyzstan Communist Party (KCP). Formed in June 1992, it was the successor to the Kyrgyz branch of the Communist Party of the Soviet Union, which had disbanded in August 1991. Akayev nonetheless was able to secure the adoption of a new constitution in May 1993. It established a parliamentary system of government with a strong executive president whose powers included the right to dissolve the parliament if that step was approved by voters in a referendum. However, the prime minister, not the president, ran the day-to-day government. Akayev was determined to make Kyrgyzstan a secular state, and he worked very hard to ensure that the new constitution did not refer to the moral values of Islam. Instead, it proclaimed Kyrgyzstan to be a "sovereign, unitary, democratic republic built on the basis of a legal secular state." Elections to the new parliament were set for 1995. In the meantime, the old legislature inherited from the Soviet era would serve as Kyrgyzstan's parliament.

Akayev's struggle with various groups opposed to his economic policies and his attempt to defend his supporters against charges of corruption—many of which were valid—soon led to changes in the country's political system. In January 1994, Akayev arranged for a referendum asking voters whether they supported his economic policies and wanted him to continue in office until the end of his term in 1995. Predictably, 95 percent of the voters supported the president. The following October, 86 percent of those voting approved Akayev's proposals for a smaller bicameral parliament. In 1995, Kyrgyzstan held its first post-independence parliamentary elections. Voters also reelected Akayev to a second term with more than 71 percent of the vote. This marked a break with what was happening elsewhere in Central Asia: During 1994 and 1995, the presidents of Kazakhstan, Uzbekistan, and Turkmenistan all had extended their terms rather than standing for reelection. Akayev chose to increase his power in another way. In 1996, he sponsored another referendum, approved by 94.3 percent of those voting, which increased presidential powers by giving him the right to appoint all government ministers except the prime minister without parliamentary approval.

During the next four years, despite economic decline and several corruption scandals, Akayev tightened his grip on power. In 1998, the Constitutional Court said he had the right to run for a third term—the constitution limited any president to two terms—because he had first been elected in 1991 under the previous Soviet constitution. Voters duly reelected Akayev in October 2000 with 74.5 percent of the vote. The election, however was marred by charges of fraud and intimidation of opposition candidates. These charges gained credibility when international observers discovered several hundred ballots that had been marked for Akayev before the balloting began. These and other irregularities led observers from the Organization for Security and Cooperation in Europe to strongly criticize the elections. As one Bishkek resident told a Western economist, who had asked about how long it took to count the ballots, "the results [of the election] were known months ago."

By 2002, Akayev faced organized opposition from a variety of sources. Aside from problems with ethnic Uzbeks in the south, he was plagued with traditional Kyrgyz clan and regional rivalries. A northerner, Akayev was caught in the old intra-Kyrgyz struggles and tensions between north and south. In March 2002, these tensions combined with objections to a border agreement Akayev made with China to create a combustible political mixture. The trouble began with large demonstrations in the southern part of the country. The demonstrators were protesting the arrest of a leading southern politician and territorial concessions Akayev had made to Kyrgyzstan's giant eastern neighbor. Five demonstrators were killed and dozens wounded. Anger over the incident simmered for months, and in November a second demonstration took place in Bishkek. Authorities arrested more than 100 demonstrators, all of whom had arrived several days earlier from the south. Meanwhile, Akayev's increasingly authoritarian style of rule had led to divisions among his own northern supporters. The president's response, in February 2003, was yet another referendum, this one establishing a new constitution with increased presidential powers. The government reported that 75 percent of the voters had voted for the constitution; opposition leaders disputed that claim, charging massive fraud in the counting of the ballots.

A further source of instability was Islamic fundamentalism. During 1999 and 2000, guerrilla forces of the Islamic Movement of Uzbekistan (IMU) were active in Kyrgyzstan. In the 1999 raids, the IMU guerrillas killed at least 18 government troops. They also took Kyrgyz police officers, four American tourists, and four Japanese geologists hostage. However, the IMU did not pose the most dangerous fundamentalist threat to Kyrgyzstan. That came from the secretive organization Hizb-ut-Tahrir, whose goal was to overthrow all the secular governments of Central Asia. By 2002, Hizb-ut-Tahrir had an estimated 3,000 active members in Kyrgyzstan, the majority of whom were operating with increasing boldness in the southern part of the country.

These difficulties were aggravated by other serious problems, among them widespread economic hardship, rising crime, and growing heroin addiction. The likelihood was that political instability lay ahead for Kyrgyzstan, especially if and when Akayev departed from the scene when his third term ended in 2005.

The Economy

The good news about Kyrgyzstan's economy after 1991 is that the Akayev government made a sustained effort to promote free market reforms. The bad news—which outweighs the good—is that the collapse of the Soviet Union dealt a severe blow to the local economy. Through the 1990s, economic decline pushed increasing numbers of people below the poverty line. At the same time, budget problems made it impossible for the government to maintain the health care, education, and social welfare networks that had provided for the population during the Soviet era. Overall, after a decade of independence, agriculture remained the basis of the economy. The most important crops included wheat, barley, potatoes, corn, and vegetables. Collective farms cultivated about two-thirds of the land, private farmers the rest. Livestock herding, though decreasing in scale, remained important, the main livestock animals being cattle, horses, and especially sheep. Kyrgyzstan's more than 4 million sheep equaled about 80 percent of the country's human population. Herders and stud farms raised about a quarter of a million tough and durable Kyrgyz horses, which for centuries have symbolized the Kyrgyz nomadic way of life.

Akayev's program of economic reform began in January 1992 with the end of price controls on most goods and services, the main exceptions being fuel, rent, social services, children's food, milk, and bread. Most of the remaining controls and government subsidies were gradually removed beginning in 1994. Privatization soon followed. It was implemented by a variety of methods including, starting in 1994, by giving every citizen vouchers that could be invested in the enterprise of one's choice. By 1997 more than 60 percent of all state enterprises were in private hands. However, that year Akayev had to temporarily halt privatization because of scandals in which state enterprises were being sold off to politically well-connected people at absurdly low prices. In one case, a silk factory in Osh was sold for barely 2 percent of its real value. In the face of strong opposition to private land ownership, in 1994 Akayev used his power of presidential decree to allow individuals the right to lease and farm land, first for terms of 49 years and then for 99 years. In 1996, he used that power to permit private land ownership; The decree took effect in 1997.

Akayev's efforts could not prevent economic decline and hardship. Between 1992 and 1995, the economy declined by 45 percent. Agricultural production fell by a third and industrial production, with Kyrgyz factories having lost many of their former Soviet markets, by two-thirds. A recovery during 1996 and 1997 was followed by further decline in 1998. While a few people became rich, unemployment in the mid-1990s was probably about 20 percent. By 2000, about 80 percent of the population was living on $2 a day or less. In economics no less than in politics, tiny Kyrgyzstan found it impossible to be an island in the vast sea of post-independence Central Asian problems.

Kyrgyzstan and the World

Kyrgyzstan's small size and military weakness have left it with little room to maneuver. One key to maintaining national security has been to seek good relations with Russia. This has included participation in the Russian-sponsored 1992 Collective Security Treaty. In December 2002, the Akayev government signed a new agreement permitting Russia to establish a military base at a military airfield a few miles east of Bishkek. Plans called for an initial deployment in Kyrgyzstan of about 1,000 Russian troops and 20 military aircraft, whose main job would be to combat Islamic militants. Meanwhile, Kyrgyzstan had acquired another powerful friend capable of balancing excessive Russian influence: the United States. In 2001, the Akayev government agreed to let the United States build its own military base in Kyrgyzstan as part of the struggle against Islamic terrorist forces operating in Afghanistan. By late 2002, that base, at the Manas International Airport northwest of Bishkek, already had more than 2,000 troops and was home to both U.S. and French military aircraft.

NOTES

p. 156 "'Oh, oh, oh, the ancient fairy tale.'" From "Fragments of the *Epos Manas* from the Version of the Great Manaschy Sagynbay Orozbakov." Available online. URL:http://www.freenet.kg/kyrgyzstan/epos.html. Downloaded December 7, 2002.

p. 157 "'our spiritual foundation, our pride . . .'" Quoted in Mike Edwards, "Central Asia Unveiled." *National Geographic*, February 2002, p. 116.

p. 157 "'Let shepherds come and hear me . . .'" Quoted in Rowan Stewart, *Kyrgyzstan* (Hong Kong: Airphoto International, Ltd, 2002), p. 50.

p. 159 "'The development of private interest . . .'" Quoted in John Anderson, *Kyrgyzstan: Central Asia's Island of Democracy?* (Amsterdam: Harwood Academic Publishers, 1999), p. 24.

p. 159 "'sovereign, unitary, democratic republic . . .'" Quoted in John Anderson, *Kyrgyzstan: Central Asia's Island of Democracy?* p. 26.

p. 160 "'the results [of the election] were known months ago.'" Quoted in Richard A. Slaughter, "Poor Kyrgyzstan," *The National Interest* (summer 2002): 60.

11

TAJIKISTAN

When the Soviet Union collapsed in 1991, Tajikistan was the poorest of its 15 union republics. Bad conditions then quickly became worse. Within months, the newly independent country nestled amid the spectacular scenery of towering mountains was plunged into a civil war that dragged on for five terrible years. The war caused an estimated 50,000 to 100,000 deaths and created approximately 1 million refugees, adding its toll in human misery to Tajikistan's severe economic, social, and environmental problems and deep political divisions. The country was turned into a Russian protectorate and Central Asia's basket case. As the 1990s ended and a new century began, the severe three-year drought that affected parts of Turkmenistan and Uzbekistan also hit sections of Tajikistan, bringing additional misery. Rains finally came in the spring of 2002. At that time more than 25,000 foreign troops—mostly Russians but also some from other Central Asian countries—were in Tajikistan, mainly to guard the country's southern border against Islamic militants based in Afghanistan. For the Tajik people, who have lived in Central Asia longer than any of their current neighbors, independence began as a grim new chapter in a history that has known more than its share of turmoil.

A Country Map

Tajikistan is the smallest country in Central Asia. With an area of 55,300 square miles (143,199 sq km), it is slightly smaller than the state of Wisconsin. The country's jagged, twisting borders give it the shape of a reindeer facing west, its slender northern section, squeezed between Kyrgyz and Uzbek territory, forming an antler tilted toward the northeast more than 150 miles in length. Tajikistan's longest border (749 miles or 1,206 km) is with Afghanistan, its deeply troubled and unstable neighbor to the south whose turmoil has seeped across the porous frontier on numerous occasions since 1991. To the west and north—and in the far north to the east as well—across a 721-mile (1,161-km) undulating border drawn to meet Soviet divide-and-rule objectives, lies Uzbekistan. Tajikistan's northern neighbor is Kyrgyzstan, except in the far west where Tajikistan's antler bends and turns so that it surrounds Kyrgyz territory on three sides, the only outlet being toward the east. Due east of Tajikistan is China, an increasingly assertive power whose imperial ambitions in Central Asia date back two millennia. Tajikistan's long, contorted borders run for about 2,268 miles (3,651 km), often through extremely rugged terrain, far too long a distance for its government to monitor and control. Given the ethnic turmoil and political instability of the region, these borders constitute yet another burden on a country whose problems far outrun its ability to solve them.

More than 90 percent of Tajikistan's territory is mountainous, half of it more than 10,000 feet (about 3,048 m) above sea level. Three of the four highest peaks in the former Soviet Union are in Tajikistan. They and others almost their equal are in the Pamir range, which covers the eastern part of the country, or in the Tien Shan ("Mountains of Heaven"), in the north along the Kyrgyz border. The highest of those mountains reflects some of Tajikistan's political fortunes in its name changes. Standing 24,450 feet (7,495 m) above sea level in the northwestern Pamirs, the mountain was called Garmo Peak before the Soviet era. When in the early 1930s Soviet explorers determined it was the highest mountain in the region, it was, not surprisingly, renamed Peak Stalin. In 1962, nine years after the brutal dictator's death, it became Mt. Communism. Finally, in 1998, the towering mountain officially was given a Tajik name: Peak Imeni Ismail Samani. The new name was in honor of Ismail Samani, a ruler (887–907) during the Persian Samanid dynasty known for his just and compassionate statesmanship.

Few people are able to eke out a living in the harsh environment of Tajikistan's towering eastern mountains. The region, covering about 45 percent of Tajikistan, is home to only 3 percent of its population. Large horned sheep, rare snow leopards, and brown bears are more at home than humans in the Pamirs. According to local legend, the Pamirs also are a refuge for the elusive yeti, or abominable snowmen, large apelike (or supposedly humanlike) creatures whose existence has never been confirmed and is not considered likely by the scientific community.

About 6 percent of Tajikistan is covered by mountain glaciers. The most impressive, almost 48 miles (72 km) long and covering an area of 350 square miles (900 sq km), is the Fedchenko Glacier, the world's largest outside the polar regions. Located in a valley more than 13,500 feet (4,200 m) above sea level, the glacier is fed by more than 100 smaller ones and provides some of the headwaters for the Amu Darya. Like other glaciers in the Central Asian mountains and elsewhere in the world, the Fedchenko Glacier has been shrinking because of global warming. It retreated about a half mile during the 20th century and on one side was separated from many tributary glaciers. Smaller glaciers in the region, or those at lower elevations or lacking a northern exposure, are in worse trouble. Hundreds of small glaciers in some parts of Tajikistan are expected to lose much of their volume or melt completely in the next 50 years. According to some experts, if present trends continue, Tajikistan will lose 25 percent of its glacial ice volume, a development that will seriously reduce the water supply throughout Central Asia.

Tajikistan's lowlands, and its main population centers, are in the northwest and southwest. The two regions are separated by mountain ranges where elevations reach about 18,000 feet (5,500 m). These mountains in turn shelter the valley of the Zeravshan River, which rises in north-central Tajikistan and flows due west for about 200 miles (316 km) into Uzbekistan, where it dies in the desert just before reaching the Amu Darya. Since the collapse of the Soviet Union, the mountains of western Tajikistan have become a major opium growing area. To their north, and therefore relatively isolated from the rest of the country, is Khudzand (population: 164,000), Tajikistan's second-largest city, and Tajikistan's section of the Fergana Valley. This region (the part that on a map looks like an antler) contains about a third of the country's population, three quarters of its arable land, and factories that produce a majority of its industrial output. It also is home to most of the country's large Uzbek minority. The southwestern lowlands, which range from about 1,640 to

3,280 feet (500 to 1,000 m) above sea level, are home to Dushanbe (population: 523,000), Tajikistan's capital and largest city. It was in Dushanbe during the spring of 1992 where clashes between opponents and supporters of the government escalated into civil war. As of early 2003, six years after the end of the civil war, the city remained a dangerous place, especially at night. It still is the scene of bombings, gun battles, kidnapings, and murders involving rival clans, political groups, or criminal gangs avenging old scores or beginning new battles.

Fast-flowing rivers tumble down Tajikistan's mountains, many ending up as tributaries of the Amu Darya or Syr Darya. The Amu Darya is formed in the country's southwestern corner at the confluence of the Vakhsh, Panj, and Kofarhihon Rivers. Together the Panj and the Amu Darya mark much of the long Tajik-Afghan border. The Syr Darya enters Tajikistan in the far northeast and cuts through Tajikistan's section of the Fergana Valley for about 120 miles (195 km) before reentering Uzbekistan. Nineteen dams have been built on Tajikistan's rivers, including the huge Nurek Dam on the Vakhsh River. There are nine major reservoirs in the country, the largest of which is behind the Nurek Dam. A major new hydroelectric dam, begun during the Soviet era but not finished because of funding problems, currently is under construction again, with the help of Russian and Iranian financing.

Tajikistan has about 1,700 lakes, three-quarters of them more than 10,000 feet (3,000 m) above sea level. The largest is Lake Karakul (Black Lake), which rests more than 13,700 feet (4,200 m) above sea level in a depression formed by a meteor about 10 million years ago. The lake is in the Pamirs near the point where Tajikistan, Kyrgyzstan, and China meet. Salty and lifeless, it is frozen and covered with snow much of the year.

Another lake in the Pamirs with much more recent origins, Lake Sarez, is best known because of the apocalyptic threat it poses to about 5 million people. The lake dates from 1911. An earthquake caused a mountain side to collapse, creating a massive landslide that dammed the Murgap River below. A large lake 40 miles long collected behind nature's new mud-and-stone dam. It is 1,500 feet high and nearly 2.5 miles wide. An international team of geologists inspected the dam in 1999 and found that it is already leaking and could collapse from another earthquake. Should that happen (the Pamirs are an earthquake zone), the floodwaters will sweep away villages not only in Tajikistan, but in Uzbekistan,

Turkmenistan, and Afghanistan. Dislodging just one cliff that already hangs precariously over the north bank of the lake alone would send a huge wall of water over the dam and probably destroy it. The floodwaters from the emptying lake, initially 300 feet high, would still be the height of a two-story building more than 600 miles (1,000 km) downstream, where they would reach the Aral Sea. It would be, one expert has said, "the largest flood on planet earth ever seen by human beings for sure." It would be much more than that. A United Nations report has warned the flood would be "the deadliest natural disaster in history."

One possible way to head off this catastrophe-waiting-to-happen is to siphon water from the lake and send it through natural and unnatural channels to the arid Aral Sea region. Such a project would help solve two problems at once: It would move water from where it is a menace and send it to where it is desperately needed. That, however, will be complicated and very expensive. It will require large amounts of international aid from organizations such as the United Nations and the World Bank.

CLIMATE

Tajikistan has a continental climate that becomes polar in the high mountain regions. Summers are warm in the subtropical southwestern lowlands, where rainfall gradually decreases as one moves southward. The Fergana region in the northwest is arid, with less than eight inches (200 mm) of rainfall per year. Most of the agricultural land in both the southwest and northwest lowland regions depends on irrigation. The most precipitation in Tajikistan is in northern sections of the Pamirs and parts of the Tien Shan mountains, where heavy winter snowfalls, often coming as fierce storms that make the mountains impassable, boost the total to more than 62 inches (160 cm) per year. That number climbs to an average of almost 95 inches (240 cm) per year by the Fedchenko Glacier. Further east in the Pamirs near the Chinese border annual precipitation is less than four inches (10 cm). The average precipitation for the country as a whole is about 24 inches (61 cm).

NATURAL RESOURCES

Tajikistan has deposits of gold, silver, aluminum, antimony, iron, lead, mercury, tin, and coal. Its gold and silver deposits are relatively large.

Tajikistan has 30 known gold deposits but has been unable to take advantage of them. The problem has been the lack of funds to develop these deposits, most of which have not even been prospected. There are also deposits of oil and natural gas that have not been developed. Tajikistan must therefore import most of the oil and natural gas it uses. More than 98 percent of the country's electric power comes from hydroelectric dams built on its fast-flowing rivers.

One natural resource that has done more harm to the country than good is uranium. During Soviet times, a secret uranium processing plant, built on Stalin's orders in the 1940s, operated in the town Chkalovsk in northwest Tajikistan. Like many other Soviet cities with top-secret military enterprises, Chkalovsk was closed to all unauthorized people. Uranium mining also took place in Tajikistan, much of the dangerous work being done by prisoners or exiles deported to the region by Stalin. The collapse of the Soviet Union brought an end to Tajikistan's uranium mining and processing. It also led to the closing of other mines, such as a coal mine in Shurab, a town further east near the Kyrgyz border. With these mines went the jobs and livelihoods of many Tajiks. All that remains in and around Chkalovsk are radioactive uranium wastes buried a few feet underground that pose a serious health threat to the local population. As one resident of the former coal-mining town of Shurab put it in December 2000, life in Tajikistan's far northwest consists of "No job, no land, no water, no hope."

People

Tajikistan's population is about 6.6 million, about two-thirds of whom live in rural areas. Ethnic Tajiks are about 65 percent of the population, while Uzbeks, the largest minority, make up about a quarter. Russians, who made up 7.6 percent of the population at the time of the last Soviet census in 1989, have declined to 3.6 percent as a result of emigration, an unstoppable trend that continues to bleed the country of many of its most educated and technically skilled people. The Russian language nonetheless still is widely used in both government and business. About 80 percent of the population is Sunni Muslim, while about 5 percent follow the rival Shia denomination. Adding to Tajikistan's many problems is its rapid population growth rate, estimated in 2002 to be 2.5 percent per year. Ironically, ethnic Tajiks in Tajikistan, about 4.3 million, are outnumbered by Tajiks in Afghanistan, where they account for a quarter of the population, or about 6.5 million people.

Culture and Daily Life

Since independence, the Tajiks have been struggling to recover their cultural heritage. Tajik culture, suffered an enormous blow in 1929 when the Soviet regime drew borders that place their traditional cultural centers of Samarkand and Bukhara in Uzbekistan. The Tajiks have lived in Central Asia since ancient times, far longer than any other major ethnic group in the region. They alone speak a Persian language, giving them the only direct cultural link to the region's first great civilization. The effort to strengthen that link has taken various forms, including honoring cultural and literary figures by placing their images on different denominations of the country's new currency, the *somoni*, issued in 2000. The honorees include Abu Abudullah Rudaki (860–941), the medieval poet

The worried look on the face of this Tajik woman at a bazaar in Dushanbe in the fall of 2001 reflects the constant hardship and tension that has gripped the country since independence. (AP/Wide World Photos/ Maxim Marmur)

THE ISMAILIS AND THE AGA KHAN

One of the more unusual groups in Tajikistan are 300,000 ethnic Tajiks who live in the Pamirs in the eastern part of the country. Known as Pamiri Tajiks, they have lived for centuries in isolated mountain villages. As a result, their local dialects are distinct from those of their lowland countrymen, who often cannot understand them. In fact, Pamiri Tajiks from different villages often cannot understand each other. However, the most distinctive characteristic of the Pamiri Tajiks is their religion. They are among the few followers of an offshoot version of Islam known as Ismaili. The Ismailis, whose roots go back to the eighth century, do not pray in mosques, have no clerics, and do not observe a weekly holy day. They are, in fact, considered heretics—that is, they are not recognized as Muslims—by both the Sunnis and Shiites. The Ismailis tend to be secular rather than religiously observant. Their spiritual leader, a man they consider a living god, is known as the Aga Khan. He lives in Switzerland, where the Aga Khan Foundation is based. During the Soviet era he was largely cut off from his followers in Tajikistan. That changed when Tajikistan became independent, and between 1994 and 2002 the foundation contributed millions of dollars to supply food and to fund a variety of projects in the Ismaili region of Tajikistan.

One of those projects with implications extending beyond the Pamiri region and Tajikistan itself is the University of Central Asia. It was established in 2000 under an agreement signed by the Aga Khan and the government of Tajikistan. The university, whose main campus is in the town of Khorog high in the eastern Pamirs, is committed to training a new educated elite that will provide creative leadership and promote democracy throughout Central Asia. Courses will be taught in English, and students will study English and computers before beginning course work towards an undergraduate degree. As one American expert participating in the project put it, "We want to give them [people in remote areas of Central Asia] the opportunity to be modern and remain where their forefathers have lived." Agreements also have been signed with the governments of Kazakhstan and Kyrgyzstan to establish campuses of the university in those countries. By 2002, planning work had begun in Kazakhstan, where it was being directed by a woman, Dr. Raikhan Sissekenova, a local public health specialist.

who Tajiks consider the founder of their poetic tradition, and Mirzo Tursunzoda (1911–77), a poet who despite living during the Soviet era worked to write down and preserve Tajik oral literature. The Tajik historian Bobojon Gafurov (1908–77) also is honored with a picture on one of the new somoni bills.

Tajikistan's most popular contemporary writer is Taimur Zulfikarov. Much of his popularity is due to his ability to appeal to current nationalist feeling by evoking the ancient Persian style of writing in his works.

Many older Tajiks still dress in the traditional way. The men wear long quilted jackets, knee-length boots, and embroidered caps, and the women wear long dresses over trousers and, on their heads, matching scarves. The local diet is similar to other parts of Central Asia, but during the hard times that have followed independence, cheaper vegetables have replaced more expensive meat.

Politics and Government

Elsewhere in Central Asia, the same political leader and supporting clique—while autocratic and repressive—has remained in power for more than a decade giving relative stability. In Tajikistan, political life has been both repressive and chaotic, the most significant event being the civil war of 1992 to 1997.

The civil war emerged from conflicts between Communists, who had run the country during the Soviet era, and a number of opposition groups with relatively little in common other than their opposition to the Communists. The Communists themselves had their own differences and varied in their flexibility and readiness to adjust to new conditions. But in 1992 they were united in their effort to exclude other political groups from political power. They were opposed by diverse groups whose ability to cooperate grew out of their common rejection of Soviet-era policies. The Democratic Party of Tajikistan (DPT) was strongly anti-Communist. It promoted secular and democratic political reforms. Rastokhez, or the Rebirth Movement, was primarily a nationalist party dedicated to the revival of Tajik culture and traditions. The Islamic Renaissance Party (IRP) was an Islamic fundamentalist group whose only use for democracy was to use it to achieve its real goal: turning Tajikistan into an Islamic dictatorship.

The first round in the long, violent, and complicated political brawl was the presidential election of November 1991. It was preceded by internal maneuvering within the Communist Party. President Mahkamov was forced to resign and Rahmon Nabiyev (himself forced from power in 1985) emerged as acting president. In late November Nabiyev won the presidency in a direct election with 57 percent of the vote. His DPT opponent, a prominent local filmmaker who had abandoned communism and ran with IRP support, took 30 percent of the vote despite complete Communist control of the media.

What followed in the next year was repression, internal Communist squabbles, and rebellion. Antigovernment demonstrations soon turned into organized attacks by armed bands. The violence grew and escalated into a civil war. In September 1992, demonstrators in Dushanbe seized Nabiyev and forced his resignation. He eventually was succeeded by Emomali Rahmonov, a former collective farm director. Russia was involved in these upheavals from the start. Moscow influenced events through troops— in particular the 201st Motorized Rifle Division (MRD), which included Russians and soldiers from several Central Asian nationalities—that had been stationed in Tajikistan during the Soviet era and after 1991 had come under Russian command. Though officially neutral, the Russian government used these troops to help the Tajik government and save it from defeat. In addition, 25,000 CIS troops (mainly Russians, but also soldiers from Uzbekistan, Kyrgyzstan, and Kazakhstan) were sent to Tajikistan. Their job was to police Tajikistan's border with Afghanistan and keep out militant Islamic forces. As of 2001, about 6,000 soldiers from the 201st MRD and nearly 20,000 CIS border troops still were in Tajikistan. Some of the 201st MRD troops were stationed in Dushanbe and in two other southwestern towns.

The Communists needed all the help they could get because they were divided into feuding clans and regional factions. Meanwhile, the pro-democracy and Islamic groups actually managed to cooperate as part of a military coalition called the Popular Democratic Army (PDA). During 1993, as the government with Russian help won control of most of the country, it banned all the major opposition groups. In November 1994, five months after peace talks began, the government held a referendum in which voters approved a new constitution. A presidential election also took place in which Rahmonov, who belonged to a southern clan, defeated a fellow Communist from a northern clan, winning 58 percent of the vote to his opponent's 35 percent. The election, marred by charges of vote rigging, was yet more evidence of the divisions plaguing the country.

In 1997, after several false starts and more broken cease-fires, an agreement between the government and what was called the United Tajik Opposition (UTO) officially ended the civil war. It also produced a framework for including the opposition in the government as the country's political system was reformed. That work would be supervised by a newly formed National Reconciliation Council (NRC), which had an equal number of members from the government and the UTO. During the next three years, Tajikistan was neither fighting a civil war nor at peace. There was constant tension between the government and the UTO, which at times refused to participate in the NRC. Assorted rebel factions, warlords, and government troops periodically fought each other. Among the political figures assassinated were a city mayor and a former prime minister, the latter having played an important role in the 1997 peace agreement. In 1998, Rahmonov distanced himself from the Communist Party of Tajikistan (CPT) and joined the People's Democratic Party (PDP). Founded in 1993, the PDP included business people as well as former Communists who were more flexible than those who remained in the CPT. In November 1999, in a typical Central Asian presidential contest, Rahmonov was reelected with 97 percent of the votes cast against only token opposition. Parliamentary elections in February 2000 were dominated by Rahmonov's DPD (64.5 percent) and the CPT (20.6 percent) amid charges by foreign observers of vote rigging. The IRP trailed with about 7.5 percent of the vote.

As 2002 ended, a very fragile peace prevailed in Tajikistan. Although the People's Democratic Party (PDP) and the Islamic Renaissance Party (IRP) both were in the government—the IRP in a minority position—in reality they were adversaries locked in an uneasy truce. Islamic militants from the Islamic Movement of Uzbekistan (IMU) and Hizb-ut-Tahrir (Party of Islamic Liberation) were increasingly active, especially in the northern part of the country near Uzbekistan. The government was espe-

Notwithstanding the use of propaganda paintings like this one to project an image of power to his fellow citizens, Tajikistan's president Emomali Rahmonov depends on Russian support to keep him in office. (AP/Wide World Photos/Maxim Marmur)

cially worried about the growing influence of Hizb-ut-Tahrir, whose reliance on propaganda rather than violence belied its fanatical goal of establishing a strict single Islamic state in all of Central Asia. In late 2002, the government cracked down on militant Islamic activity by closing a fifth of the mosques in one northern district. This raised tensions that already were high, largely because the Islamic Renaissance Party saw the crackdown directed at itself as well as the IMU and Hizb-ut-Tahrir. Overall, there were few signs suggesting the prospect of political stability in Tajikistan.

The Economy

Tajikistan's economy was in trouble during the final decade of the Soviet era. After 1991, the Tajik economy was hard hit by the disruption of the former Soviet trading system, which had tied it both to Russia and the other former Soviet republics. In addition, the economy was battered by the civil war. All this turmoil and misfortune caused the economy to decline by an average of 16 percent per year between 1990 and 1996. It did not begin to recover until the civil war ended in 1997. That recovery did little for most of the Tajik people. According to most estimates, as of 2002 about 80 percent of the country's population lived below the poverty line.

Agriculture accounts for a third of Tajikistan's economy while employing 45 percent of the work force. Most of the country's irrigated land is devoted to growing cotton, its most important crop and its second largest export. Tajikistan also grows grain, vegetables, potatoes, and fruits such as grapes and watermelons. Its most important industry by far is aluminum smelting. The Soviet regime built one of the world's largest aluminum smelters in the southwestern Tajik town of Tursunzada, near the Uzbek border. This gigantic enterprise consumes 40 percent of Tajikistan's electric power. It employs 12,000 workers and overall supports 100,000 people. However, after independence Tajikistan was unable to import the raw materials the plant needed, and production has remained at about half of capacity. Still, that is a lot of aluminum, most of which is exported, making aluminum Tajikistan's number one export. The plant also accounts for about a quarter of the Tajik government's total revenues.

At the same time, the Tursunzada aluminum smelter may be Tajikistan's worst polluter. Each year it spews into the atmosphere hundreds of thousands of tons of poisonous hydrogen fluoride, sulfur dioxide, nitric acid, and other pollutants. These pollutants have damaged orchards, vineyards, and fields in the region. The milk and meat of local farm animals is not fit for human consumption. A common sight in the region are cows with missing teeth. Human health has suffered as well. Among the problems are increased birth defects and blood and endocrine disorders. Both sides of the Tajik/Uzbek border have been affected.

Economic reform has come slowly to Tajikistan. Although some small state-owned companies have been sold, medium and large enterprises and collective farms remain in government hands. Overall, the future is not promising.

NOTES

p. 168 "'the largest flood on planet earth . . .'" Louise Hidalgo, Quoted in "Major Flood Fears for Tajik Lake." BBC Online Network. June 18, 1999. Available

on-line. URL: http://news.bbc.co.uk/1/hi/world/asia-pacific/372386.stm
Downloaded December 23, 2002.

p. 168 " 'the deadliest natural disaster in history' " Quoted in "Tajikistan Mountain Lake Poses Potential Disaster." Dispatch Online, December 29, 1997. Available on-line. URL: http://www.dispatch.co.za/1997/12/29/page11.htm. Downloaded December 23, 2002.

p. 169 " 'No job, no land, no water, no hope.' " Quoted in *The New York Times*, December 19, 2000, p. A3.

p. 171 " 'We want to give them . . .' " Quoted in *The New York Times*, August 16, 2002, p. A2.

CONCLUSION

As of 2003, after more than a decade of independence, Central Asia was a region with enormous problems and generally grim prospects. Few of the problems that had plagued the region in 1991 were being dealt with successfully, and many were becoming worse. While the severity of particular political, economic, and social difficulties varied from country to country, a cloud of disappointment and failure covered the region. The vast oil and natural gas reserves of Kazakhstan and Turkmenistan held the promise of future economic prosperity in those countries, but far-reaching political and economic reforms were needed to make that promise a reality for the overwhelming majority of the population. Although the governments of Turkmenistan, Uzbekistan, and Tajikistan certainly were worse than those of Kazakhstan and Kyrgyzstan, all were authoritarian and corrupt. Domestic problems within the borders of each country were made worse by transnational factors. Most of the world's heroin, en route to markets elsewhere, passed through Central Asia, corrupting governments and daily life, creating addicts as it went. Islamic fundamentalism, despite a series of recent setbacks, remained a destabilizing force and a potential threat to most of the regimes in the region, especially in light of widespread poverty and corrupt secular governments that seemed incapable of creating conditions under which life could improve. Continued turmoil in Afghanistan to the south and outside pressure from countries like Russia, China, and Iran were additional sources of instability. Neither the will nor resources existed to begin dealing with the disastrous environmental damage caused during the Soviet era.

Tajikistan was the region's basket case. Although its civil war officially had ended in 1997, in reality Tajikistan was coming apart at the seams. The government's authority did not extend beyond Dushanbe, the capital, and the country's borders were being policed by soldiers operating under Russian control. According to a World Bank report issued in 2002, 83 percent of the country's people were living in poverty. Tajikistan was what political scientists call a failed state: a country where the central government in effect does not function and social and economic institutions consequently are in a state of collapse.

Kyrgyzstan, while better off than Tajikistan, was also on the verge of becoming a failed state. This was both ironic and especially sad because in 1991 President Akayev, the only Central Asian president who was not a Communist Party functionary during the Soviet era, had been committed to free-market economic reform. At that point he even seemed to favor democratic political reforms. But over the next decade the impact of economic decline far outweighed any positive results from economic reform. While he certainly was not a Niyazov or Karimov, with each passing year Akayev began to look less like a Western democratic leader and more like an old Soviet party boss and traditional Central Asian despot. By 2003, Kyrgyzstan was deeply in debt, dependent on foreign aid, and increasingly under the influence of Kazakhstan, its huge neighbor to the north.

Turkmenistan was something of a bad international joke. It had great potential riches because of its natural gas reserves, but it also was under the thumb of an egomaniacal dictator whose policies were ruinous. Any real progress clearly would have to await President Niyazov's departure from office, whether by natural causes, given his questionable health, or by virtue of a political coup.

Uzbekistan was a milder but decidedly more powerful version of Turkmenistan. With the largest population in Central Asia, and with significant Uzbek minorities in several neighboring states, Uzbekistan was a rival both to Russia and Kazakhstan for influence in the region. Its natural resources, if properly developed, potentially provided the basis for future prosperity. However, Uzbekistan also languished under a corrupt dictatorship that was committed mainly to maintaining itself in power, closing the country to foreign influences, and delaying meaningful economic reform. That did not add up to a promising future.

Despite some setbacks and a growing U.S. presence in Central Asia, Russia continues to wield considerable influence in the region, as illustrated by this July 2002 meeting between Russia's president Vladimir Putin (second from right) and (from left to right) President Askar Akayev of Kyrgyzstan, Islam Karimov of Uzbekistan, Nursultan Nazarbayev of Kazakhstan, and Emomali Rahmonov of Tajikistan. (AP/Wide World Photos/Itar Tass)

In 1991, Kazakhstan began its life as an independent state with the best prospects of any country in Central Asia. It had enormous undeveloped reserves of both oil and natural gas, and therefore was a magnet for international investment. Its president, Nursultan Nazarbayev, despite his past as a Communist Party official during the Soviet era, had a reputation as a reformer and was regarded both at home and abroad as competent and forward-looking. But Nazarbayev, while encouraging international investment and promoting some economic reform, also became increasingly authoritarian and corrupt. The story in Kazakhstan during its first decade of independence was not entirely negative, especially in terms of economic performance fueled by oil exports. At the same time, by 2003 it was clear that Nazarbayev and his associates were incapable of providing Kazakhstan the leadership it needed to solve its most pressing social and economic problems.

Central Asia thus began the 21st century in a very difficult situation. The best that could be said is that for the first time in centuries it was independent of outside control. It held its future in its own hands. Whether that would make things better or worse than before was an open question.

CHRONOLOGY

Ancient Times to 1700

500 B.C.

Persian Empire at its height

329 B.C.

Alexander the Great conquers the Persian Empire

323 B.C.

Alexander the Great dies shortly after leaving Central Asia

Late fourth century B.C. to mid-third century B.C.

Seleucid kingdom

Mid-third century B.C. to third century A.D.

Parthian Empire

Second century B.C. to third century A.D.

Kushan kingdom

First century B.C.

Start of Silk Road and Chinese presence on eastern fringe of Central
 Asia

Third century

Revived Persian Empire under Sassanid dynasty

Fourth and fifth centuries
Hun invasions

Sixth century
Turkic tribes become established on northern Central Asia steppe

640s
Arabs conquer Sassanid Persian Empire

Early eighth century
Arabs conquer parts of Central Asia, including Samarkand and Bukhara, bringing Islam to the region

751
Battle of Talas: Arabs defeat the Chinese

Ninth century
Persian Samanid dynasty

10th century
Turkic invaders destroy the Samanid state

973–1048
Al-Biruni

980–1037
Avicenna

11th century
Seljuks invade Central Asia; are followed by other Turkic invaders

13th century
Mongol conquest

1370–1405
Conquests and rule of Tamerlane

1409–1449
Rule of Ulugh Beg

16th century
Kazakhs established on northern steppe of Central Asia

17th century
Uzbek states control southern Central Asia

Russian Central Asia:
Eighteenth Century to March 1917

1718
Russians build a fort at Semipalatinsk on the Kazakh steppe

Mid-18th century to 1820
Russians consolidate control of Kazakh steppe

1838–1845
Unsuccessful Kazakh rebellion against Russian rule led by Kenisary Qasimov

1865
Russians take Tashkent

1867
Russians take Bukhara

1868
Russians take Samarkand

1881
Russians take Goktere fort

1888

Russian railroad reaches Samarkand

1897

Russian-British agreement creates the Walkan Corridor ("Afghan Finger")

1905

Revolution in Russia fails to overthrow the czar; Russian railroad reaches Tashkent

1906–1912

Large numbers of Russian and Ukrainian settlers establish farms in Kazakhstan

1911

Earthquake in Tajikistan causes landslide that creates natural dam on the Murgap River, forming Lake Sarez

1914–1918

World War I

1916

Kazakh rebellion against Russian rule

March 1917

Revolution in Russia overthrows the czar

Soviet Central Asia: November 1917 to 1991

1917

November 7: Bolsheviks overthrow the Provisional Government

1918–1920

Civil War between Bolsheviks and the Whites

1918

Basmachi Revolt begins

1918–1919

Famine in Central Asia

1922

Bolsheviks kill Enver Pasha

1922–1923

Bolsheviks defeat most Basmachi rebels

1924

Uzbek SSR and Turkmen SSR established: Kazakhs, Kyrgyz, and Tajiks receive autonomous republics

1929

Stalin consolidates power; Tajikistan SSR established; collectivization begins: leads to mass starvation in Central Asia over next five years

1931

Central Asian production makes Soviet Union self-sufficient in cotton

1932

Collectivization completed in Central Asia: one-fifth of Kazakh population homeless.

1932–1933

Terror Famine in Ukraine and parts of European RSFSR

1936

Kazakh SSR and Kyrgyz SSR established

1936–1938

Stalin's Great Purge sweeps Soviet Union

1937
Soviet Union becomes an exporter of cotton

1938
Faisullah Khojaev tried in Moscow and executed as a subversive

1940
Cyrillic alphabet replaces Latin alphabet for writing Central Asian languages

1941
June 22: Nazi Germany invades the Soviet Union, bringing the Soviet Union into World War II

1943
February: Soviet Army wins the Battle of Stalingrad

1945
May 9: End of World War II in Europe

1948
Earthquake levels Ashgabat in Turkmenistan, killing 100,000 people

1949
August 29: Soviet Union tests its first atomic bomb at Semipalatinsk in northeast Kazakhstan, the first of 456 nuclear tests (116 in the atmosphere) at that site

1953
Stalin dies

1954
Soviet leader Nikita Khrushchev launches Virgin Lands project

1956 and 1958
Bumper wheat harvests in the Virgin Lands

1959

Garagum Canal begins operation, drawing water from the Amu Darya

1959–1983

Sharaf Rashidov Communist Party boss in Uzbekistan

1962

Muynoq, the southern Aral Sea port, on a peninsula instead of an island as Aral Sea retreats

1963

Drought and poor farming techniques turn Kazakh steppe into a dust bowl

1964

Khrushchev removed from office; Leonid Brezhnev becomes Soviet leader

1964–1986

Dinmukhamed Kunayev Communist Party boss in Kazakhstan

1970

Muynoq completely surrounded by land as Aral Sea retreat continues

1979–1988

Soviet military intervention in Afghanistan

1982

Brezhnev dies

1985

Mikhail Gorbachev becomes Soviet leader; Saparmurad Niyazov becomes Communist Party leader in Turkmenistan

1986

Gorbachev replaces Kunayev with Gennadi Kolbin as Kazakhstan party boss

1988

Birlik (Unity) Uzbek nationalist group founded in Tashkent

1989

Gorbachev replaces Kolbin as Kazakhstan party boss with Nursultan Nazarbayev, an ethnic Kazakh; Uzbek mobs attack Meskhetian Turks in Fergana Valley in Uzbekistan; Uzbeks and Tajiks clash in Tajikistan; Islam Karimov becomes Communist Party leader in Uzbekistan

1990

Democratic Kyrgyzstan movement founded; Bloody Uzbek-Kyrgyz riots in Osh in Kyrgyzstan; Karimov chosen president of Uzbekistan by parliament; Nazarbayev chosen president of Kazakhstan by parliament; Askar Akayev chosen president of Kyrgyzstan by parliament; Niyazov, running unopposed, elected president of Turkmenistan with 98.3 percent of the vote; Kahar Mahkamov chosen president of Tajikistan by parliament

1991

March: Central Asian voters strongly support continuation of the Soviet Union in national referendum
August: Unsuccessful coup against Gorbachev
December 25: Gorbachev resigns as president of the Soviet Union
December 31: At midnight, the Soviet Union officially ceases to exist

Independent Central Asia: 1991–the present

1991

August: Kyrgyzstan and Uzbekistan declare independence
September: Tajikistan declares independence
October: Turkmenistan declares independence; Akayev, running unopposed, elected president of Kyrgyzstan with 95 percent of the vote
November 24: Rahmon Nabiyev elected president of Tajikistan with 57 percent of the vote
December 1: Nazarbayev, running unopposed, elected president of Kazakhstan with 98.8 percent of the vote

December 16: Kazakhstan declares independence

December 21: Commonwealth of Independent states founded in Almaty

December 29: Karimov elected president of Uzbekistan with 86 percent of the vote

1992

Kazakhstan: Signs Strategic Arms Reduction Treaty (START)

Uzbekistan: New constitution introduced

Turkmenistan: Niyazov, running unopposed, is reelected president with 99.5 percent of the vote

Kyrgyzstan: Adopts new constitution

Tajikistan: Civil war begins

1993

Kazakhstan: Signs Treaty on Non-Proliferation of Nuclear Weapons (NPT)

Uzbekistan: Press brought under government control; independent media outlets outlawed

Turkmenistan: Niyazov takes title "Turkmenbashi" ("Leader of the Turkmen")

1994

Kazakhstan: U.S. airlift removes weapons-grade uranium from the country

Uzbekistan: People's Democratic Party of Uzbekistan (PDPU) and other Karimov supporters win all seats in parliamentary elections

Turkmenistan: 99.99 percent of voters participating in referendum approve extension of Niyazov's presidential term to 2002

Tajikistan: Voters approve new constitution; Emomali Rahmonov elected with 58 percent of the vote in election marred by fraud

1995

Kazakhstan: Last of Soviet-era nuclear weapons removed from the country; Nazarbayev's presidential term extended to 2000 in voter referendum; new constitution strengthens presidential powers; elections marred by irregularities give Nazarbayev supporters control of parliament

Uzbekistan: 99.9 percent of voters in referendum approve extending Karimov's presidential term until 2000

Kyrgyzstan: Akayev reelected president with 71 percent of the vote; three-day festival celebrating the 1,000th anniversary of epic poem *Manas*

1996

Uzbekistan: Karimov resigns from the PDPU, saying he wants to be nonpartisan; new law bans all political parties organized on ethnic or religious basis; museum honoring Tamerlane opens in Tashkent; Daewoo builds $640 million automobile factory in Fergana Valley

1997

Turkmenistan: Niyazov has quadruple cardiac bypass surgery in Germany

Tajikistan: Civil war ends

1998

Uzbekistan: Uzbek exiles in Afghanistan found the Islamic Movement of Uzbekistan

Turkmenistan: Economy ends decline and begins to grow; new natural gas pipeline running through Iran begins operation

Kyrgyzstan: Constitutional Court rules Akayev can run for a third presidential term

1999

Kazakhstan: Nazarbayev reelected president with 80 percent of the vote; Akezhan Kazhegeldin, a leading opponent of Nazarbayev, leaves Kazakhstan for exile in Europe; Karmat steel mill finally earns a profit

Uzbekistan: Bombs kill 15 people in Tashkent, apparently as part of plot to assassinate Karimov, who is unhurt; Turkish company opens factory to build cars and minibuses in Sarmarkand; Niyazov declared president for life

Tajikistan: Rahmonov reelected with 97 percent of the vote; geologists inspecting the natural dam holding back Lake Sarez find it is leaking

Kyrgyzstan: IMU guerrillas battle government troops and take hostages

2000

Kazakhstan: Irina Petrushova founds *Respublica*; U.N. report shows 65 percent of the population lives in poverty; 89 percent of those voting approve new constitution that further strengthens presidential power

Uzbekistan: Karimov reelected in two-man race with 91.9 percent of the vote; economy recovers to 1991 level; IMU guerrillas infiltrate across southern border and battle government troops

Kyrgyzstan: Russian made second official language; Akayev reelected to a third term

Tajikistan: University of Central Asia established; amid charges of vote rigging, parliamentary elections dominated by People's Democratic Party

2001

Kazakhstan: Two leading pro-democracy advocates imprisoned; economy grows by 13 percent as foreign investment flows into oil and gas industries

Turkmenistan: Niyazov publishes *Rukhnama* (Spiritual Rivival)

Uzbekistan: U.S. troops arrive as part of military campaign against the Taliban and al-Qaeda; 90 percent of voters approve extending Karimov's term to 2007

Kyrgyzstan: Military agreement with the United States permitting a U.S. airbase near Bishkek

2002

September 27: Central Asian states agree on treaty establishing Central Asian Nuclear-Weapon-Free Zone

Kazakhstan: *Respublica's* offices firebombed; daughter of opposition newspaper editor murdered

Uzbekistan: Signs security agreement with the United States as U.S. aid climbs to $160 million per year; Daewoo automobile plant in Fergana Valley makes first profit

Turkmenistan: Days of the week and months of the year renamed: January becomes Turkmenbashi; unsuccessful attempt to assassinate Niyazov

Kyrgyzstan: Anti-Akayev demonstrations in March leave five dead and dozens wounded; a second protest demonstration in Bishkek in

November; military agreement allows Russia to establish military base near Bishkek

2003

Kyrgyzstan: Voters approve a new constitution that increases presidential powers

FURTHER READING

Allworth, Edward, ed. *Central Asia: 130 Years of Russian Dominance, a Historical Overview.* 3d ed. Durham and London: Duke University Press, 1994.

Allworth, Edward A. *The Modern Uzbeks: From the Fourteenth Century to the Present.* Stanford: Hoover Institution Press, 1990.

Anderson, John. *Kyrgyzstan: Central Asia's Island of Democracy?* Amsterdam: Harwood Academic Publishers, 1999.

Bremmer, Ian, and Ray Taras, eds. *Nations and Politics in the Soviet Successor States.* Cambridge and New York: Cambridge University Press, 1993.

Curtis, Glenn E., ed. *Kazakstan, Kyrgyzstan, Tajikistan, Turkmenistan, and Uzbekistan: Country Studies.* Washington, D.C.: Federal Research Division, Library of Congress, 1997.

Hostler, Charles Warren. *The Turks of Central Asia.* Westport and London: Praeger Publishers, 1993.

Knobloch, Edgar. *Monuments of Central Asia: A Guide to the Archaeology, Art, and Architecture of Turkestan.* London and New York: I.B. Taurus Publishers, 2001.

Macleod, Calum, and Bradley Mayhew. *Uzbekistan: The Golden Road to Samarkand.* Hong Kong: Odyssey Publications, 1999.

Melvin, Neil J. *Uzbekistan: Transition to Authoritarianism on the Silk Road.* Amsterdam: Harwood Academic Publishers, 2000.

Olcott, Martha Brill. *Kazakhstan: Unfulfilled Promise.* Washington, D.C.: Carnegie Endowment for International Peace, 2002.

Rashid, Ahmed. *Jihad: The Rise of Militant Islam in Central Asia.* New Haven and London: Yale University Press, 2002.

Roy, Olivier. *The New Central Asia: The Creation of Nations.* New York: New York University Press, 2000.

Smith, Graham, ed. *The Nationalities Question in the Post-Soviet Successor States.* 2d ed. London and New York: Longman Group, 1996.

Soucek, Svat. *A History of Inner Asia.* Cambridge and New York: Cambridge University Press, 2000.

Steward, Rowan, with Susan Weldon. *Kyrgyzstan.* Hong Kong: Airphoto International, 2002.

INDEX

Page numbers followed by *m* indicate maps, those followed by *i* indicate illustrations, and those followed by *c* indicate an item in the chronology.